NOT A SOMETIMES LOVE

God's richest blessing to you! — Keith Korstjens

KEITH KORSTJENS

GREEN KEY BOOKS

Holiday, Florida
www.greenkeybooks.com

NOT A SOMETIMES LOVE

International Standard Book Number: 0-9705996-1-7

Cover Art: Mike Molinet

Printed in the United States of America

All Scripture quotations, unless otherwise marked, are from the King James Version of the Bible. Scripture quotations marked *(TLB)* are taken from *The Living Bible*, copyright ©1971. Used by permission of Tyndale House Publishers, Inc., Wheaton, IL 60189 USA. All rights reserved. Scripture quotations marked RSV are taken from the Revised Standard Version of the Bible, copyright 1952 [2nd edition, 1971] by the Division of Christian Education of the National Council of the Churches of Christ in the United States of America. Used by permission. All rights reserved.

For information:
GREEN KEY BOOKS
2514 ALOHA PLACE
HOLIDAY, FLORIDA 34691

Library of Congress Cataloging-in-Publication Data available upon request.

2/5/23

IT BEGAN WITH A VAGUE FEELING—A FEELING OF "COMING DOWN WITH SOMETHING." TWENTY-FOUR AGONIZING HOURS LATER, THE LIVES OF TWO PEOPLE HAD CHANGED FOREVER.

On a warm Saturday morning, Keith Korstjens rushed his wife, Mary, a normally healthy, active twenty-four-year-old, to the hospital. That "vague feeling" had developed into a high fever and the fear that it might be "something really serious." On that day, Keith Korstjens was told his wife of three years had polio—she would spend the rest of her life as a quadriplegic.

Forty-six years later, Keith Korstjens has a story to tell and retell—the story of his and Mary's life together since that day, working to build a marriage in a world of respirators, wheelchairs, braces, and bedpans.

Living with a handicap is never easy. Keith Korstjens is frank about the low times—the long hours of soul-searching and resentment, the moments of heart-wrenching frustration, the times when the million small indignities and inconveniences came to seem too much.

But there were also triumphs—and surprises. Mary's first success at feeding herself after a hundred tries and failures. Moments of exquisite tenderness as they found ways to recover sexual intimacy. Times of laughter over the eccentricities of the various housekeepers. Feelings of satisfaction as they each developed special ministries that used their gifts and talents. And the quiet thrill of discovering, over and over again, that no matter how unlovable and resentful and defeated we may feel, God's love for us never falters!

Not a Sometimes Love is an enormously refreshing love story—from start to finish it rings true in its testimony to faith, hope, and love. It's a book you will read with tears in your eyes and a smile on your face. And if you are one of those who feel worn down by the constant pressures of your commitments, it may give you just the encouragement you need to keep your love alive and growing.

to my Mary,
the one person above all others
who has made the Word a living reality before me!

contents

before you begin

had just finished packing my bags. Ken had packed his things, too, including his rods and reels. We were going to be away from one another for several days, I on a speaking engagement and he on a fishing trip. We had only been married a few months, and we knew we'd really miss each other.

Wheeling through the living room that afternoon, I was surprised to see a beautiful red rose in a bud vase on the table. That Ken! Really thoughtful. Moving into the bedroom to gather my things, I spotted *another* rose in a bud vase on my dresser. I glanced in the bathroom and to my amazement yet *another* red rose adorned the counter.

By the third rose, my excitement turned sour. It wasn't that I didn't appreciate his gifts, it's just that…well, both he and I were ready to leave. Nobody but our miniature Schnauzer, Scruffy, would be in the house to enjoy the flowers. *Expensive* flowers at that, I pointed out.

Ken smiled and waved me off.

As I traveled to that speaking trip, I thought of the quality that marks the ministry of love. It is *extravagance.* Love is extravagant in the price it is willing to pay, the time it is willing to give, the hardships it is willing to endure, and

1

the strength it is willing to spend. Love never thinks in terms of "how little," but always in terms of "how much."

This is the kind of love that has marked my marriage to my husband, coming up on almost 20 years. With my quadriplegia—I became paralyzed in a diving accident in 1967—my husband has learned to think in terms of "how much," not "how little." It has been two decades of deep commitment, but also deep disappointments. Fun and laughter, but also anger and frustration. Yet the dark threads have been woven in with the light ones to create a unique and binding relationship between Ken and me. Perhaps, the most poignant and loving times are those when Ken has had to go the extra mile to help me cough when I'm sick or blow my nose when I'm sad. Truly he is one awesome guy!

And now, when Ken and I speak to other couples who live with a disability at our Joni and Friends Family Retreats, we are able to share the kind of advice we gleaned when we first married. We are able to point people to this book, *Not A Sometimes Love*, written by our friends, Keith and Mary Korstjens. Truly, the book you hold in your hands was the first marriage manual we ever read, and my husband and I, to this day, are still practicing the advice and holding fast to the insights we learned twenty years ago from *Not A Sometimes Love*.

Love gives, love knows, and love lasts. Love always thinks in terms of "how much." And this is the sort of love God has given us. The quality that marks the ministry of the love of our Savior is the sheer extravagance of giving...and giving again. When the Father considered ransoming sinful men and women such as ourselves, I don't think he thought in terms of how little He should give, but *how much*. This is the pattern for marriage. It is not a 50%-50% proposition between a husband and wife; it is 100%-100%. It is each giving and giving again!

By the way, when I returned home from that speaking trip, I got an added surprise. Those little buds were in full bloom, brightening my home with their extravagance and a lingering fragrance of love. It is my prayer that as you read *Not A Sometimes Love*, you will discover the art of loving as God loves and giving as He gives.

Keith and Mary, after many years of marriage with a disability, have perfected this incredible art. And you can, too.

Joni Eareckson Tada
President, Joni and Friends

acknowledgments

Many people have assisted in the development of this book. I am indebted to all for their valuable contribution. Ideas were often refined in the spirited conversations in the Duetts Class of the First Baptist Church of Pomona, California, and the principles that emerged were tested in the life experience of loving friends.

The encouragement to even attempt the writing came from Joyce Landorf. Without Joyce's assurance the book would probably never have been written. She also spent priceless hours reviewing and refining the manuscript.

I owe so much to patient, lovely women who typed and retyped the earlier writing. Jan Grizel, Florence Mellard, Sherry Figueroa and Sheila Rapp all gave such loving assistance in typing.

Without Anne Buchanan's and Robin Hardy's editorial skill, so much would have been lost. My deep appreciation goes to them and to all the others named above whose affirmation and encouragement made the book possible.

introduction

Everyone has a handicap of some kind. That immediately puts us all on the same level. Some of us just have the kind of handicap that we can hide rather nicely. There are no braces or crutches or respirators. Our handicaps are deep inside. No one is particularly conscious of them until they burden some relationship. For example, no physical handicap could ever be more damaging or limiting to relationships than a dwarfed emotional makeup. A disposition arrested in emotional growth at age seven or nine creates far greater havoc in attempts at human intimacy than the loss of a leg, the inability to move an arm, or a slight hesitation in speech.

Yet hundreds, perhaps thousands, who have found themselves physically impaired have convinced themselves that, for them, the full range of normal relationships with people can never again be a reality. They have emotionally withdrawn from friends and loved ones; they have developed lopsided attitudes that suggest the world now owes them a living because of their personal disaster, or they have developed a "devil-may-care" bravado that hides an inward sense of deep inferiority. How pathetic, how unnecessary is their pained isolation.

This is the story of a remarkable woman who hasn't just risen above a handicap—she has capitalized on it! She's remarkable partly because she doesn't think of herself as at all unusual. When she talks about herself, it's always in terms of being a most ordinary lady. Yet she has given to me—her husband—some of life's greatest gifts as she has lived out a winner's lifestyle...from a wheelchair!

It's also the story of what we have learned together about the most wonderful, the most perplexing, the most rewarding of all human relationships—marriage. Our marriage has grown and deepened and sweetened every one of those many years since our personal little "disaster." It hasn't happened *in spite* of Mary's handicap. No indeed. It has happened *because* of it.

We're excited about what we've learned. Somehow, we want everyone else to get in on it, too.

Recently, a friend from San Diego, Houston Burnside, was telling about the ordeal of his son's struggle to regain movement and a sense of personal usefulness after a devastating paralysis had left him almost totally immobilized. Houston said his son, who had known Mary for a number of years, kept repeating to himself throughout the ordeal, "If Mary could do it, I can do it! If Mary could do it, I can do it!"

Perhaps because Mary *did* do it, you can do it!

Keith Korstjens
Claremont, California

8

the day that changed our lives

That summer had been one of the busiest we had known. Even with only three years of experience as a young fledgling minister, I couldn't believe the pace we had set. We were worn to a frazzle. Youth camps had kept both Mary and me busy through the hot, dry months of summer. Fall had skidded into our awareness like a hotrod doing a tight turn in a dusty lot. Suddenly, it was October. Two weeks of an evangelistic effort in our church required our physical presence each night at the church buildings. Gradually, we sensed just how drained and exhausted we were.

The next week began like so many others. Monday was my day off from work. I puttered in the yard and made some repairs to the window screens of the three bedroom house we were renting. Tuesday my wife, Mary, felt as though she were coming down with something. Her pale, clear, bone-china complexion was flushed and oddly set off against the background of her dark brown hair. We arranged to have our two small children, Kenneth, three years old, and Karen, a year and a half, stay with some friends in the church. It would be better, we thought, to have them out of the house rather than catch something from Mary. Thursday,

Mary was almost sure she had the flu, so she went to the doctor's office. She had a little fever but not much else. The kindly Christian doctors, husband and wife, who cared for our family were not much concerned. "We'll just keep an eye on this for a day or two," they remarked.

I didn't want to catch the flu any more than I wanted my children to get it, so I slept in Kenny's bedroom the next couple of nights.

Saturday of that week changed our lives. Mary awakened before me, as usual. She has always been a "day person." It used to frustrate me to no end that she could bounce out of bed in the morning and be going full speed by the time her feet hit the floor. I'm a "night person." In the morning, I stagger from the bed, grope my way into the bathroom and fight my way to consciousness somewhere between shaving and brushing my teeth. When Mary awoke this Saturday morning, however, she didn't lunge out of bed as usual. She softly called to awaken me. When I stepped in from the other bedroom, she said in a small, quiet voice, "I think there's something the matter with my shoulder. I can't seem to raise myself up on that side." I looked at her in disbelief as she attempted once more to raise up on her elbow, but instead crumpled into the mattress, totally unable to support her weight on her right side. I helped her dress without yet completely comprehending the growing clumsiness that had overtaken her.

As we got into the car to drive to the doctor's office, I was not aware of something that was now taking over Mary's thoughts. There was a growing apprehension on her part that something was *seriously* wrong. Once inside the doctor's office, the brief examination he gave her seemed to cause no alarm to the male doctor of the husband-wife team. It was thought best, however, to arrange for a spinal tap to be taken at the local community hospital. We were to go there immediately. As we started out the door, Mary mentioned to the woman doctor how uneasy she felt about all of this. Somehow she felt that something was seriously wrong! At this, alarm spread across the face of the woman doctor. "This is one of the positive symptoms," she said. Then with great hesitation, she brought herself to disclose to me her temporary diagnosis. "I think Mary has polio," she said finally. "It is the anxiety that Mary senses that is the key." Such a simple little thing as a casual remark going out the door had provided insight to the doctor.

Before the days of the Salk vaccine, cases of polio were common enough among adults, but it was one of those remote things that happens "to other people." Besides, poliomyelitis was more commonly known as infantile paralysis. It was thought to be primarily a childhood disease. The fact that former President Roosevelt had suffered severe paralysis during his adult years in no way made the possibility of personal encounter with the dreaded disease more likely in my mind. It just didn't seem possible! This wasn't happening to us. It was all a crude mistake, a simple misjudgment on the part of an otherwise competent and loving Christian doctor.

At the emergency room of the hospital, they took immediate charge of Mary. They swept her away and left me standing in a waiting room. Without a word to me, the nurses put her on a gurney and rolled her quickly away through the double doors. I didn't have the vaguest idea that I would be spending the longest six hours of my life in that room. Those hours were the closest thing to hell I have ever experienced.

No one came to bring information about Mary. I was strangely alone in the room that afternoon. The hours dragged by as I made feeble efforts to occupy myself. There were three magazines in the rack. I thumbed through each one and then went back to read each one from cover to cover. Still no word about Mary. I paced the floor. That pale green room became oppressive. Feelings of desperation began to mount. Throughout the six hours, no one made any effort to inform me of the progress of the tests that were being made and the necessary care being given to my wife behind those awesome double doors. My imagination ran wild.

Polio! What was it like? I knew so little about it! Was it fatal? How do you contract it? Did Mary really have it? Would I see her again? What if she died behind those doors, and I wasn't even there with her? "Oh, God," I cried out, "what can I do? Nobody will tell me anything. I've got to know *something*—anything! Please, God, help me! I don't think I can stand it if this goes on much longer!"

Maybe that doesn't sound very "spiritual." Maybe a young minister should have more faith than that. Perhaps. But at that moment, the whole of my world was behind those double doors, and I wasn't even thinking about faith, or trust, or anything else so "spiritual." I feared that I was about to lose the girl I loved. My world was collapsing, and in a moment, I hurled myself upon God's mercy. Actually, that was probably the greatest act of faith in my entire life!

For in that moment of abandon, I allowed God to do the one thing I needed more than all else—to give me His peace.

My world was collapsing... I hurled myself upon God's mercy.

Almost in moments after I prayed it happened. It was as though God, for the moment, anesthetized all my emotions. I felt entirely calm and at ease. Deep down inside I was at rest. Even though I had no idea what was going on behind those forbidding doors, at least for that moment I somehow knew inner quiet and certitude. It was only much later that I began to comprehend just what God had done for me there in that hospital waiting room.

Then very shortly a nurse appeared through the doors. She asked crisply, "Are you Mr. Korstjens?" I replied that I was. With no effort to be gentle or reassuring, she simply blurted out, "Your wife has polio. She may not live." And then she disappeared through the doors again! That confirmation sounded surely like a death sentence for Mary! Even the inner peace that I had momentarily known was overshadowed by that announcement, and I lapsed into shock. Much of what took place in the following moments I do not remember at all. Mary and others at the hospital pieced it all together later.

Mary was placed in immediate isolation, for polio is a highly contagious disease during the first days of onset. High fever and delirium are often present. The next incident that Mary recalls may have been a figment of a delirious mind, or it might have been frighteningly real.

13

Mary remembers being in the hospital room, and that I entered briefly, fully gowned and masked to guard against contagion. I stood across the room from her and spoke. She longed for me to come to her and hold her, even for a moment. She felt so miserable and alone and frightened. When she called to me to come, I only stood at a distance and could not respond. She was crushed and hurt. There was no way for her to comprehend that I could not come to her! Now she was alone.

Mary's limbs were rapidly becoming useless from the kind of polio known as spinal poliomyelitis. At the same time, her ability to breathe and swallow was decreasing at an alarming rate as a second kind of the dreaded disease, called bulbar, overtook her respiratory system. Emergency surgery was scheduled to do a tracheotomy on Mary. The only surgeon available was called from a dinner party where he had been drinking heavily. His alcohol-laden breath nauseated Mary as he bent over her. The surgeon clumsily opened her trachea and inserted a stainless steel tube in the opening. Air was pumped into her lungs through this tube to keep her alive until a respirator could be readied for her. Then she was placed in an iron lung, a huge tanklike affair, that actually began to "breathe" for her. Its rhythmic movement, alternating between pressure and vacuum, artificially activated her body's breathing mechanism and drew precious oxygen into her lungs.

At this point, I remember that from somewhere a nurse materialized. Totally unlike the cold, unfeeling harbinger who had appeared earlier, she spoke gently to me, "Your wife is in isolation, but you can see her through the window if you will go outside on the lawn next to the building. Her room is the third one on the east side of this wing. You will have to go back out through the emergency room and make your way around to the back of the hospital. We can't allow you now to go through the contagion ward." If there were people in the emergency room by now, I was not aware of them. Eager to be with my Mary, I ran out into the evening and tried to find the contagion ward from the back of the hospital grounds. I wasn't exactly sure what to look for. I ran from window to window of the first building I came to, searching for her room. When each in turn proved to be the wrong one, it dawned on me eventually that I had mistaken the location of the ward and was searching the wrong wing.

I sensed the panic of a small boy lost in a strange place. Uncertainty and terror brought feelings of desperation and isolation. I needed Mary, if only to be near her, but I couldn't find her. With fresh, hot tears blurring my vision, I stumbled across the lawns to another wing. Down the east side I went, bumping into a post, thrashing through shrubbery, past one window, then another, finally to the third.

Then I found her!

Peering through the screen, I was shocked to see her encased up to her neck in a mechanical monster. Somehow, no one had thought to tell me that polio victims needed the "tank," as it was called, to keep them alive. I was just barely able to see the reflection of her face in the mirror over her head. The look on her face was one of helpless bewilderment, as though she couldn't believe all this was really happening to her. I was doubly dismayed to make out the bandages and tube in her throat. She was fevered and hardly

15

coherent by this time and probably not even aware of my presence at the window. I simply stood there crying. Never had I felt more helpless than I did that day.

I stayed pressed against the window screen as long as the nurse would allow. Finally she closed the window. I was shut out.

Numbly, I wandered back to the lobby of the hospital and inquired about visiting hours. It occurred to me that I should telephone someone. I called Harry and Evelyn Warren, the friends who were keeping Kenny and Karen. Though I don't remember how, I must have choked out some kind of a message about Mary's illness. Evelyn said that the children could continue to stay at their house for awhile. I wasn't to worry about them she told me. She and Harry would take them to Sunday school and church the next morning.

I searched the back of my pocket datebook for the telephone numbers of my parents and Mary's mother and daddy. Again, I have no memory of the ordeal of breaking the awful news to either set of parents. But Mary's folks, who lived in San Diego, said they would come the first thing in the morning to take charge of the children. Mary's daddy was a tender, thoughtful man who was a deeply-committed Christian. He prayed with me on the telephone, asking God for strength for me.

A long, torturous night followed. I went home to the darkened, empty house and tried to sleep, but that was impossible. I wept and prayed through the long hours until morning.

The next day was Sunday. Before the grandparents returned to San Diego, we all attended services at the church where I was the Minister of Christian Education and Youth. During worship, an usher came to whisper to me that Kenny, who was in the nursery with his little sister, Karen, was not feeling well. As I bolted from my seat, my mind was obsessed with the awful fear that my son was also victimized by the terrible disease. I rushed into the nursery, only to find Kenny lying flat on his back in a playpen, listless and flushed. I scooped him up into my arms and was sure that my fears were confirmed as I felt his hot face next to mine. High fever. Surely, he had polio, too.

Another trip to the doctor's office and a hurried admittance to the hospital followed. Driving to the hospital with Kenny, I was stricken with terror. Somewhere out of the depths of an agonized soul, I *pleaded* with God for my son! Torn between terrible fear for my little boy's very life, and feeling angry and hostile toward God who let all this happen, I was alternating between bitterness toward God and feelings of total helplessness and fear.

At the hospital the examination and cursory tests were accomplished with surprising speed. This time the doctor herself came out to tell me the results. "Kenny is sick, all right. But it's nothing we can't handle. He just has a kidney infection. He's going to be well in no time at all. If you can, have someone keep Kenny in bed for a few days and the infection will be licked." Relief swept over me at the news, but that relief was followed quickly by a sense of awful humiliation. Only an hour or so before, I had been remonstrating with God, telling Him how angry I was that He would permit my son to become ill. I had felt totally alone and helpless, almost denying in my own self that God even cared! I had to go to the Lord in humiliation. "How could I have ever believed such a thing of you, God? I'm really pretty faithless and stupid! God, forgive me!" Believing with all my heart that moment that God would not even consider me fit for the ministry any longer, I was ready for Him to speak from Heaven in judgment and banish me. What came, instead, caught me totally unprepared. God said simply and quietly within my mind, *"It's all right. I understand about your feelings. Trust me in this, too!"* The relief that came to me was overwhelming. I felt helpless in my immaturity before God as I wept freely, yet I was His son! I had virtually shaken my fist in the face of God in anger, yet I was forgiven! I was empty, yet I was full! Many times in the long years that followed, I knew the same, ineffable cleansing and filling of the Spirit of God.

As I stumbled through the next few days, I gradually awoke to the realization that God had been so very carefully upholding me, steadying and strengthening me through all this nightmare. I was just beginning to grasp both the magnitude of the situation and what God was doing about it. However, I could not as yet accept the whole thing.

Mary was only twenty-four. She was bouncy and full of energy. Everyone just naturally thought of Mary when there was a job to do. She was the kind to get it done! It didn't matter if it was cooking dinner for twenty-seven kids in the youth choir or making fancy centerpieces for the tables at the mother-daughter banquet. Mary was always in the thick of the activity. Her dedication to Christian service was coupled with a delightful, childlike joy in just being and doing.

We had been married only four years, and our babies were still so little. All of life was still out before us. How could this be happening to me, a minister, and to Mary, a committed Christian girl? How could God be allowing her to be totally paralyzed? This didn't make any sense. Surely, it was a mistake, and God would rectify it! "O God," I prayed, "please heal my Mary! I know I don't have any right to come to you for special favors, but please, God, don't make her go through this. She's so young! Her whole life is before her. Fifty years of lying paralyzed and motionless and kept alive by a machine . . . O God, that's just not fair! Lord, I'll even take her place if you'll only make her well!"

I searched frantically in the Bible for passages that spoke about divine healing. I read and reread those words, hoping to find some guarantee that Mary could be made well again. I think I even felt a little bit that if I could only find something in the Bible that was really "air tight" about promising healing to everyone, then I could pressure God just a little bit to come to her rescue. Motives are hard to trace in moments like that. You grasp at *anything* that might serve your purposes.

Well-meaning friends would say to me, "Keith, just *claim the promises!* That's all you have to do. God will do the rest!" At home again that night, I would open my Bible to the now familiar passages: "He was wounded for our trans-gressions, he was bruised for our iniquities: the chastisement of our peace was upon him; and with his stripes we are healed" (Isaiah 53:5); "Come, and let us return unto the Lord: for he hath torn, and he will heal us; he hath smitten, and he will bind us up" (Hosea 6:1); "For I will restore health unto thee, and I will heal thee of thy wounds, saith the Lord" (Jeremiah 30:17). As I read many passages like these in the Word, I wondered why God didn't answer my prayers for Mary's healing. It all seemed so plain. Then I would read words like, "Jesus said unto him, 'If thou canst believe, all things are possible to him that believeth'" (Mark 9:23); "'And all things, whatsoever ye shall ask in prayer, believing, ye shall receive'" (Matthew 21:22); "The prayer of faith shall save the sick, and the Lord shall raise him up" (James 5:15a). Was that it? Was the problem that I didn't have enough faith? I thought to myself, "Who are the people I know who really have faith? I'll ask them to pray for her!" So I said to my pastor, Dr. Miles Dawson, "I need your help! I need people who can *really believe* who will pray for Mary with me. Will you help?" I went to Nathan Carr, chairman of our Board of Deacons. "Nathan, will you add your faith to mine and pray for Mary's healing?" The young man who was our assistant pastor, recently out of seminary and filled with eagerness and faith, seemed like a good comrade to enlist. "Jay, will you and Priscilla get a hold of God on Mary's behalf and pray for her healing? I need your faith. My faith alone just isn't strong enough to bring a miracle of healing!"

But Mary wasn't healed.

Then, I enlisted the prayers of everyone I knew to pray for her healing. Perhaps, if I could storm the gates of Heaven, God would hear and answer! If enough people were praying, perhaps then God would *have* to heal her. Still, Mary was not restored.

Gradually, as the time lengthened into weeks and then into months, I began to understand more fully the complete teaching of the Word of God about divine healing. It didn't depend upon my degree of faith. Even the Apostle Paul was not granted healing from a physical malady with which he was beset. He had earnestly pleaded with God on three different occasions that it be removed, he says in 2 Corinthians

"Just trust me, Keith. Trust me!"

12:7–9, but God had said to him simply, "My grace is sufficient for thee," and the sickness or malady remained. It didn't depend upon Mary's faith, for some in the New Testament had been healed completely *without* faith demonstrated on their part. When Jesus healed the man who had been born blind, as the incident is recorded in John's Gospel, chapter nine, Jesus said the healing was "that the works of God should be made manifest in him" (v. 3), and he healed him without any apparent demonstration of faith on the man's part at that time. When Jairus came to Jesus asking for new life for his daughter, Jesus brought her back from the dead! She didn't exhibit any faith. She couldn't!

I came to see, too, that healing was not "in the atonement," as some had suggested to me, reading Isaiah 53:5 as a proof text. Healing is entirely up to God! *He* would decide in His perfect knowledge of things if healing and restoration were the best thing for Mary. Through all of this, He kept saying to me, "Just trust me, Keith. Trust me!" I desperately wanted to do that, but my heart wouldn't let me...not yet. I was to find the gentleness and wisdom of God in the hundreds of little pieces of the answer to my question, "Why?" before I could fully trust Him in this.

21

Before God could fit all those pieces together for me, I suppose it was somehow necessary for me to get to know *Him* a lot better. How easy it is—even for a minister—to know a lot *about God* and not know Him very well. During those long, hour-and-a half trips to Rancho Los Amigos Hospital, where Mary was soon transferred, I had plenty of time to get to know God. He and I talked a lot. Maybe that's where I really learned to pray. People tell me often they are moved when I pray aloud. That always startles me just a little. I don't exactly know why my prayers are any different from others except that maybe God has become more real to me than to most.

Thirteen months of coming home to an empty house made me well aware of the joys of having someone there to greet me. I found every excuse for not going home at night. Just a light in the house anywhere would have been a welcome sight. Some months later, when Mary's aunt was there for a few weeks, it seemed so good—so warm and comforting—to come up the driveway at night and see the lamp shining in the big living room bay window. No wonder families who must be separated from each other at times learn to put a light in the window to welcome the traveler home. Nothing—absolutely nothing—says, "Welcome home!" like a lighted window.

Loneliness was a hard thing to fight. It dogged my steps. During the day, I had to keep constantly busy. Even though I was surrounded by other members of the church staff where I was employed and by dozens of young people in the youth departments I supervised, I was painfully *alone*. At night I tossed and turned, frequently unable to sleep at all. The bed next to me was empty, and I was agonizingly aware that I was alone. I kept telling myself that I should be able to "get a hold of God" in all this. He would be my companionship. I didn't need to feel loneliness. But telling myself that didn't always work. There were times that I needed someone there to hold, "someone with skin on," as the saying goes. When I felt embarrassed before God for not being satisfied with His presence alone, He gently helped me to the realization that the feelings I had were only the full validation of my humanness. He had put me together that way, with the very needs I was sensing. God wasn't a bit chagrined over my need for human companionship.

That experience of loneliness has helped me identify so many times with the many "formerly marrieds" now in our church family here in Pomona. Their nights of loneliness are real. The lack of the physical presence of a loved one now gone—either because of death or divorce—is sensed in an overwhelming way. Even when one thinks inwardly that God should—and will—provide that needed companionship, it's just not that easy to escape the haunting, gnawing grip of loneliness.

Mary's period of isolation at the hospital lasted for about two weeks. From the very beginning she had to have "special" nurses, that is, individual nursing care around the clock. During those first two weeks she had nearly twenty different nurses as efforts were made to try to find capable and adequately trained nurses with experience in handling respirator patients. Every day there was someone new and strange to care for her personal needs. Sometimes, it was a little scary for her.

One nurse showed up one evening thoroughly drunk. As I stood outside Mary's window singing softly to her, the tipsy duty nurse joined in at the top of her lungs on the hymn "The Old Rugged Cross." A little later that evening she became convinced that Mary was hallucinating. She called the doctor to the room. When he observed who, indeed, was hallucinating, she was removed from duty.

With the frightening experience of having so many strangers care for her who often knew little about the real terrors of being in the tank—or out of it for even a few seconds—it was not so strange that when late one night Mary awoke to find a beautiful blond nurse standing nearby, she greeted her with, "Are you an angel?" The nurse turned out to be an angel of sorts. She was gentle and thoughtful, a delightful Christian girl whose husband was studying for the ministry.

After the isolation period, Mary was moved into a larger room called a solarium. Another polio victim who also needed special nursing was placed in the same room. That provided the two "specials" with some assistance from each other as they took care of every personal need of their patients. Removing a polio victim from the iron lung, or tank, even for a few minutes to bathe her, is frightening for the patient. Both nurses could team up on such efforts and reduce the time needed to keep the patients out of the tank. But in order to be out, Mary had to first learn to tolerate what was called positive pressure breathing. In this process, a tube was connected to her trachea tube and air pumped directly into her lungs. Getting the trick of cooperating with such a machine instead of fighting it wasn't easy! Even trusting it to do for her what the big iron lung did was difficult.

Polio victims say about this step in their therapy program, "You know in your head the machine will do it, but to trust your life to it is something else!" This breeds its own brand of fear as you wonder after each breath if it will be the last you will ever get. Other steps in the rehabilitation program are equally fearful. When Mary was first submitted to being away from the tank *and* positive pressure both, it was terrifying! They were attempting to teach her to breathe again on her own using a different method of drawing air into the lungs. Actually, she finally learned to breathe almost in the reverse of the way others normally breathe. At the beginning, however, she would experience panic as she felt unable to get air into her lungs. That made the learning process all the more difficult. We both knew that this sense of panic must be overcome.

...when we were totally at the end of ourselves... God gave victory over the panic.

We prayed...oh, how we prayed! God showed us that this, too, was unrelated to any lack of faith on our part. What wonderful deliverance that was! So many people, including Mary and me, have believed that if only you "have enough faith," then everything is going to be all right. When everything is *not* all right and you still experience panic, the immediate conclusion is that something is amiss in the area of your faith. How inadequate and guilty one then feels! For a young minister to sense this was devastating. God gently instructed us about faith. We began to see that we didn't have to generate "enough faith." In fact, when we were totally at the end of ourselves, then God gave victory over the panic. It was His promised gift of faith. Treatment for polio victims can take many forms, depending upon their personal physical involvement. While attempting to re-educate another set of abdominal muscles to breath for Mary, the therapists also began other forms of respiratory therapy. For instance, they attempted to teach Mary "frog breathing." This is a system of gulping air, so called because it gives the patient a frog-like appearance at first until the skill is mastered. Then the whole thing can be done without even attracting attention. They failed miserably at that, though. Or at least, someone failed. Mary never did learn to frog breathe. After that came the "rocking bed." This is an ingenious bed device that actually rocks up and down from foot to head. The patient lying on the bed experiences the thrust of the rocking motion putting gentle pressure on the diaphragm, pushing it up and allowing it to fall in rhythmic motion. When she got used to the rocking bed, it was a delight to Mary. She could be out of the tank and free to begin using some of the muscles in her legs that the physical therapists had so laboriously restored to partial usefulness by this time. Being able to move *any part* of her body after weeks and weeks of paralysis was cause for celebration.

But this was all pretty hard work. Mary often knew physical exhaustion. Lying on the rocking bed as I came in at afternoon visiting hours, she would often have a drawn, tired look in her eyes—eyes that usually snapped and sparkled. She never openly complained, but occasionally her conversation betrayed that her body was so tired she felt she really couldn't go on. Frequently, she was discouraged from seeming lack of progress. When she couldn't learn frog breathing, she was depressed. These taxing efforts of learning to breathe again and the physical and emotional exhaustion they produced left Mary with only one source of inner strength—her Father in Heaven. A simple childlike faith now kept her one day at a time. Reaching 'way back into childhood, she recalled verses from the Bible that she had memorized in Sunday school. She repeated them to herself over and over. From them, she gained strength. And in the midst of her own struggle, she began to find ways of reaching out to other women there in the ward.

Maxine, next to her, lay wishing each day simply to die. Her husband had driven down from Idaho to be with her during hospitalization. But the attraction of a pretty hospital attendant proved too much for immature love. Just as Maxine was about to be dismissed to go home, her husband deserted her for the pretty attendant whom he thought could better fulfill his physical needs. Then, there was no home to which she could go!

Millie Buttons had given up everything dear to her five years before. When she had been admitted to the hospital with severe paralysis from polio, she had tearfully told her husband and one little girl goodbye. Feeling physically inadequate to meet his sexual needs now and unable to offer the two of them her care, she had suggested they find a new life without her. Incredibly, her husband had followed her suggestion!

Out of the reservoir of strength gained from those Bible verses, Mary began to reach out emotionally to Millie. She reassured her daily of God's incredible love for her person-

27

ally. She comforted and lifted Millie's spirits when depression dropped a damp, dark, hideous shroud over her delicate countenance. Finally, hope, a sense of personal worth, and the will to live gradually began to reappear in Millie. Her own progress of recovery began to quicken. She began to take an earnest interest in her own therapy program. Her appetite improved. A smile and laughter escaped from her lips now on occasion. Years later, we learned that Millie—who had felt she had nothing to give her husband—had published a book of beautiful poetry. There, in the salvaging of a life, was one of the hundreds of pieces of the answer to our question of "Why?" about this terrible illness.

Looking back on all this after years of ministry in which I have lived through the pain and struggles of hundreds of my parishioners, I understand now that God doesn't deliberately inflict such things upon His own. God didn't "send" this illness to Mary. He's not like that! The inner anguish I had often felt, plus the pain of so many others, had driven me back to the Bible again and again to try to comprehend. In the midst of my own struggle for meaning here, I had found why God had included the story of Job in His Word. People have always searched for the meaning to suffering. There, in the terribly human story of Job, God lets us all see that it is the nature of life on this planet that causes suffering—not an act of God. When a beautiful, talented child dies, it isn't God who "takes the child." When a young, Olympic-bound skier suffers a tragic, crippling accident and is forever snatched from competition and glory by that one, awful moment, it isn't a capricious God who has hurled the skier into oblivion by one act of whimsy—it is life! Life that brings suffering and agony to the rich and the poor, the talented and the mediocre, the good and the not-so-good.

"He doth not afflict willingly nor grieve the children of men," reminds Jeremiah in his lament (3:33). The Apostle Paul picks up the theme in the New Testament hundreds of years later and says, "All things work together for good to them that love God, to them who are the called according to his purpose." (Romans 8:28) It is true that God takes even evil and turns it into good—if we let Him! When faced with suffering and tragedy, we always have two choices. On the one hand, we may choose to withdraw, become embittered, and die inwardly ourselves, or we may choose to reach out to God in whatever way we know and say to Him, "God, how can I work together with you to help turn this senseless, awful thing into something good?" In that sense, there is a human side to Romans 8:28. Because Mary was willing in her uncomplicated, childlike way to *let* God do something, He began to turn her tragedy into good.

The months of her hospitalization and treatment, the excitement of three-hour "passes," and visits three times a week to a hospital more than an hour and thirty minutes away, all had a way of changing our lifestyle. However, when Mary came home right after Thanksgiving the next year, we were hardly prepared even yet for the changes it would mean.

For instance, there's that convenient little device known as a bed pan. We had made limited use of one on passes from the hospital; I had even pitched in and assisted the busy nurses in attending Mary at the hospital on occasion. But a bed pan partly filled with urine is in a different league from a bed pan after a laxative. And I'm the fellow who used to have trouble rinsing out dirty diapers when our two kids were yet in plastic pants. There were times when nausea nearly layed me out. If Mary had not long before relinquished any semblance of personal modesty at being nursed at the hospital and in its place developed a hearty sense of humor about her personal needs and care, we scarcely could have survived. She helped me laugh at the bed pans and at myself.

But a wonderful sense of humor doesn't handle everything. Mary was no superwoman, either. Some things really "got to us." I remember one afternoon when our three-year-old Karen came running into the house with a skinned knee. The most natural response of a mother is to reach down and gather her injured child into her arms. A Band-Aid and a little T.L.C. can make almost any scratch well. But for the first time it hit Mary with crushing force—she could not stretch out her arms and lift little Karen to hold her tight. Those arms were useless. Little Karen stood crying beside her mother's wheelchair, not fully understanding why Mommie didn't hold her and comfort her. That was hard for a mother to handle! I watched the episode...and wept too.

One evening when relatives had come to visit, they were showing movies taken of the family on much earlier occasions. A sequence picturing Mary before her illness, and still able to walk, filled the screen. Little Karen exclaimed, "That's my 'nother Mommie. She can walk!" Somehow, it still hadn't penetrated into that little one that this was her only Mommie, and that she would never walk again.

How do children make the transition from before to after? Through the tears of frustration on the part of a brokenhearted mother who can no longer lift her crying little one to hold her tight. Sometimes, through acts of special tenderness that only such a mother can devise. Because Mary was always at home when the children needed her, they soon learned that they could climb up into her lap in the wheelchair, even though she could not lift them there. When Karen would do just that, taking Mary's useless arm and literally *holding* it around herself for comfort's sake, Mary learned to make the most of those tender moments. She discovered how to fill them with love and warmth. She taught them, consoled them, read to them, sang with them, looked at the magazines with them, told them Bible stories, and did a hundred things more...never moving from the wheelchair. When it was impossible to enfold them in her arms, she wrapped them in love. When she could not do the little things she longed to do, she taught them how to do for themselves. Patiently, she instructed them with simple words about tying shoelaces, about hanging dresses and trousers, about setting the table, about all the things a mother teaches a small child—and never was she able to show them how!

Sometimes children make the transition from before to after with impish testing of their newfound situation. Karen was the mischievous one. She learned early that Mary could not leave the chair to punish her when she was naughty. Sometimes she would stand just an arm's length or so from Mary with an impish grin, as though to say, "Yah, yah, you can't catch me!" But then, as Mary verbally corrected her, she would begin to feel the pangs of conscience, and lie down on the floor in front of the wheelchair to allow Mary to "spank" her with her one good foot. She couldn't have felt the gentle pats on her little bottom, but she howled in anguish and put on a good show!

Sometimes the transition is through growing tenderness on the part of a handsome, big-for-his-age, young son who soon developed a protective air about his mother. Sometimes Kenny would come in from play and make a beeline for Mary to be sure that she was comfortable, that there was nothing lacking in her provision. On rare occasions when he found his mother in tears, he would caress her hands and face and say soothingly, "It's all right, Mommie. We'll take care of you!" Hearing her four-year-old speak so knowingly to her fear, and seeing him stand so tall and straight as her protector and provider, caused her to smile gently, even through her tears.

That gentleness and tenderness remained in the inner life of that boy. Years later, attending a high school football awards banquet, I was seated next to Kenneth's coach. He commented to me, "Ken could be a great football player—he's got the size [6 feet tall and 210 pounds] and the speed. And he's probably smarter than most of the kids on the field. But he's too gentle. He'd rather outsmart that other lineman than hit him hard. He's just not enough of a tiger!" There was no way I could tell that coach how valuable that gentleness really was, or of what price it had been born.

It's funny how much we take for granted the little items of everyday. Like a fork or spoon, for instance. Mary couldn't manage an ordinary fork at first. So the occupational therapist developed what was called a "spork" for her. A "spork" is a combination spoon and fork. It's a cleaver device that is made so no matter at what angle you hold the handle, the rest of the implement remains level. Where the bowl of the spoon would normally be, the spork also includes the tines of a fork. It's a handy gadget for the paraplegic or "quad" just learning to feed himself again. Yet even this ingenious mechanism cannot make up for the concentrated effort needed to learn to utilize it. Learning its use is a trial and error, attempt and fail, try and try again kind of experience. Mary and I found out this kind of learning experience isn't one-sided at all!

"There, I think you've got hold of it okay," I'd observe as I slipped Mary's hand through the strap on the handle. "Let's see how you do with the mashed potatoes."

"I'm going to do it today," Mary would say with determination. "Just watch me!" She would swing the arm tray back and with intense concentration swing forward, holding the spork with all the tiny grip she could muster. Both backward and forward motions of the arm tray supporting her forearm were accomplished by movement originated by trunk muscles of the upper body. The spork would swing awkwardly forward, aimed at the mound of mashed potatoes...and miss. The effort would be repeated again without success. Finally, after the attempts became labored and Mary was already showing signs of fatigue, the spork and potatoes would make contact. Then began the tortuous process of lifting the pathetic little amount on the spork up to her mouth. More often than not, the potatoes slipped from the spork and fell back to the plate.

While this heroic effort was in progress, I would try to be encouraging. "Oops, missed that time, but you'll get it this next time! That's it, you got 'em that time...hurray for you!"

The greatest victories in life are sometimes simple things...

When the potatoes were precariously ensconced on the spork, Mary would look up with obvious pride on her face, her eyes sparkling. Then the whole attempt sometimes would crumble as the contents of the spork dropped to the plate, and with it the sparkle of achievement in Mary's eyes. Now there would be disappointment, sometimes even tears.

The greatest victories in life are sometimes simple things, like just being able to get the potatoes into your mouth! I remember the smile of triumph when Mary mastered mashed potatoes.

But with this, as with many other ventures, we discovered how really amazing is the structure of the human body. There are actually several ways to breathe, using different sets of muscles in the body. It is only a matter of reeducating those muscles to do different tasks than before. It is the same with activating the arm. With no arm muscles available to Mary, muscles in the trunk of her body were taught to swing that arm and tray forward and back, up and down. The psalmist who said "I am fearfully and wonderfully made" said only the half of it!

By the time Mary was dismissed from the hospital to come home for good, she was breathing with the aid of a device known as a chest respirator. The unit that powers it is a portable machine that can create an adjustable vacuum pressure within a shell-like apparatus worn over the upper-front abdomen. It looks like a giant turtle shell, but Karen aptly named it Mommie's Big Tummick! Each time Mary was in a prone position the shell and machine had to be in operation. If there was a temporary power failure or even the slightest interruption of current, a loud warning bell sounded. Otherwise, the rhythm of sixteen pulsations a minute to correspond with her breathing pattern soon became a part of the process of falling asleep each night. Learning to operate this machine, being trained to use a suction machine to clear the open trachea of mucus, fitting arm and leg braces to helpless limbs—all these were a new world for us with daily victories and frustrations. And there were other battles yet to be mounted!

feelings, fears, and phantoms

Life behind the wheels of a wheelchair was to be an entirely new experience for me. I really was not prepared for the feelings and fears that I would face nor the phantoms that would overtake and haunt me.

All during the time of Mary's hospitalization, I kept assuring her that everything would be okay when we were together at home again. We would handle it. I even had myself fairly well convinced during those months. Time and again, we talked and planned for "going home."

"We'll have to have a special electrical circuit installed for the machine, Honey," Mary suggested. "And the power company will have to be alerted to keep us on 24-hour emergency standby in case of a power failure."

"Yes, I can take care of that all right," I responded, thinking to myself for the first time, *What will I do if we do have a power failure in the middle of the night?*

I paid a little closer attention to the training I was receiving in the emergency operation of all Mary's equipment. Occasionally, I found myself waking up at night with a start, as my mind was going over the checklist of things to do in a crisis. At times, I found myself really afraid that something would go wrong and that I wouldn't be able to handle it.

Now, finally at home, disquieting questions began arising in my mind. Try as I would to not think about them, they crept relentlessly back into my awareness.

Can I really "pull off" this thing of being a faithful husband? What would happen if I started feeling differently about Mary now that we are home? Suppose our sex life could never get going normally again? How would I handle that?

I feel that I love her, but am I sure? Suppose it is only pity, and I am just feeling honor-bound now to care for her? Would that be enough to keep our marriage together?

How long can I actually carry on taking care of practically all of her personal needs of bathing, toileting, and everything without becoming resentful of these demands on my time?

I kept telling myself that it was idiotic to think about things like that. I felt guilty for even entertaining such questions. Yet they persisted. They *demanded* an answer—each one!

I had to face them, and as I did, something came to me. I believe it was a special word from my Heavenly Father, "Don't be afraid of the questions! Never try to evade your doubts. Having questions and doubts is never sinful, for facing these doubts and fears head-on is the only way to gain assurance about anything."

"Do you mean it's okay, God, for me to have these crazy thoughts?" I asked.

"It's not only okay, but I will even use them to bring greater strength to your love for Mary and your marriage in days ahead," He replied. "Yours will be a love and marriage that will endure. You will *know* it's for real when you've come through this crucible of refining.

"By the way," He continued, "you'll find the answers to those questions as you live one day at a time. Don't expect to have answers to them all by the day after tomorrow."

"Yours will be a love and marriage that will endure."

So the questions persisted over a period of time, but as He had said, experience answered them better than logic or argument.

With all of this came a myriad of changes in daily lifestyle. There was hardly any way to prepare for them. Even the brief months in the hospital before Mary was dismissed, when she was already in a wheelchair some of the time, were no real preparation for living every day, all day, with someone who could not even get out of the chair without assistance.

The hospital wisely attempted a program of preparation. Several weeks before Mary was dismissed to come home permanently, she was permitted to leave the hospital from time to time on a "pass."

The staff at the hospital knew from experience that when patients leave the hospital for the first few times, they frequently experience panic and desperation, sometimes for no apparent cause at all. So the first "pass" they arranged for Mary was for three hours.

When the news came through "channels" that Mary was going to be allowed to leave on her first pass, she could hardly wait to tell me at my next visit on Tuesday night. "We can leave for three whole hours, and do anything we want!" she told me, as excited as a little girl on Christmas Eve. We began to plan whom we could get to come with me to drive the car so that I could give full attention to Mary's needs. We decided to ask Jay Schmidt if he could drive his station wagon for our exciting first trip away from the grounds.

It seemed wise to bring his station wagon instead of my sedan. Mary had not yet achieved what is called a "standing transfer" from bed to chair in which she could be helped to a standing position and stay up long enough to turn and sit. So, she had to be lifted bodily from one place to the other. We reasoned that we could lift her from the bed to a chaise lounge with the aid of the hospital's hydraulic bedside lift. Then, we could wheel her directly to the station wagon on the lounge. Also, the lounge would allow Mary to be in a semiprone position and use the portable respirator to assist in breathing.

So, on the Saturday of the pass, I arrived with borrowed station wagon and chauffeur. We excitedly gathered together Mary's equipment. There was the portable respirator, the cumbersome battery pack to supply electrical power, a suction machine to keep the trachea clear of mucus and finally, the chaise lounge on which we would transport Mary herself. Altogether, it was an impressive array of equipment! Except for the lounge, every piece had to be listed on the checkout sheet with the charge nurse of the ward. Finally, we were rolling Mary and respirator down the hall to the outside door. We were actually going to leave the hospital! Mary hadn't been out of the hospital since she had been admitted several months before.

I was feeling almost giddy with excitement. Mary experienced mixed emotions. She was naturally ebullient over the prospects of this adventure, but at the same time hesitant, fearful. In a small, childlike voice she said, "Oh, Keith, stay close to me! What if we can't make it?"

"We'll make it okay," I answered, holding her hand to reassure myself as much as her. We were beginning the attachment one forms to that which is "safe." It grows as one is totally dependent upon others for sustaining life itself, and it was coming through to us with clarity now. Venturing out from the safety of the known hospital procedures on one's own can be an act that requires great courage.

I needed to learn just how much courage was required. It is not a simple thing to understand the feeling that goes with never being sure that you will be able to draw another breath into your lungs. I tried to empathize by doing silly little exercises like exhaling as much breath as possible from my lungs, then going as long as I could without breathing in. But that was a futile exercise—I always knew that I could just inhale at any moment when my body cried out for oxygen. How different to have the body systems screaming for oxygen to the lungs! That's when panic seizes one in an icy grip. The fear is deep—and real—and no one who has not experienced it can ever empathize. Try as I might, I could not... *really*.

However, these first passes were to teach me a little about fear.

As we wheeled down the long green corridor of Ward 501, I talked reassuringly to Mary. "Aren't we fortunate that the clearance came through for this weekend, when Jay could be available to help! We have his station wagon out in the parking zone at the back of 501." As we passed the first few rooms on either side of the corridor, other patients called out, "Good luck, Mary!" "Have a wonderful time." "Don't worry, Mary, everything will be okay!" Word always travels swiftly in the hospital ward about anyone who is attempting the first pass. Some who had already gone for their first such experience wanted sincerely to be reassuring. They had known the same feelings Mary was now sensing as we neared the door. *They* could empathize with panic and fear. Would I ever be able to really enter into this, or would I forever remain an outsider, unable to help, unable to grasp?

Sometimes the hardest task of all for the one who is at the side of the ill or handicapped is that of handling the discovery that you cannot do anything but stand there. Inwardly you long with desperation to assume something of the illness, the pain, the handicap—but you can't! You cannot ever really feel what they are feeling.

Once outside the building, we carefully positioned the chaise lounge at the rear of Jay's station wagon. Still attached to her battery-powered, portable respirator, we lifted Mary— chaise lounge and all—into the station wagon. It must have looked a little like the television series "Emergency," except that we wore no paramedic uniforms and were considerably more clumsy!

Jay gently wheeled the station wagon about and headed toward the boulevard. Mary was lying on the chaise lounge in the back. What we had not counted on was that this placed her face within just a few inches of the ceiling of the wagon. It seemed so stuffy and close in there to her! She began to sense just a twinge of uneasiness.

Trying to go over in our minds to be sure we had remembered everything, Mary suddenly exclaimed, "Oh, Keith, we forgot the pan!" A bed pan! How could we have overlooked that?

"There's a big Thrifty Drug Store down a little way. We can stop there and I'll get one. We'll have it for use at home later on!" I thought I had dispatched that little problem neatly, but I didn't count on the emotional weight that forgetting a simple item could carry. Mary was thinking, *What if we have forgotten something really important? We won't be able to get what we need in time. I might not be able to make it.* She began to sense mounting panic. Though the machine was carrying out the necessary movements for her to breathe, she felt there was not sufficient air inside the auto. We made it about three more blocks down the street before she was crying in desperation. Try as she did to fight the fear and panic, she dissolved into tears. We turned around and fled back to the hospital. The three-hour pass had lasted about twenty minutes.

When we returned to the hospital ward and she was once more within the safety of the familiar, reassuring procedures, she gradually regained her composure. In the process, however, she could not refrain from tears of remorse. She felt she had failed. Worse, she felt she had failed *me*! "Oh, Honey," she cried, "I made such a mess of it! I didn't want to blow it all...I wanted it to be fun for you. I'm so sorry!

We were going to be *together*—just us—for the first time in such a long time, and I couldn't do it! Can you forgive me?"

I couldn't believe my ears! All this time I had been certain I had done something wrong somewhere and mishandled something badly. Surely, she would have been able to make it if I had been more helpful, reassuring, proficient. I was in tears by now, holding her and asking her forgiveness for being such a clumsy idiot. We must have presented a strange picture to Jay and the others standing around.

Something began in a tiny way that afternoon that has since grown to become an intrinsic part of a sturdy, lasting marriage. We sensed, if only so incompletely that afternoon, how much we had to depend on each other now. If our marriage, even our lives, were to survive it would be only by developing an unusual interdependence. Little by little over the years the significance of that has unfolded.

It wasn't until just before our second attempted pass some weeks later that I learned that Mary had never been on battery-powered equipment before that Saturday. No wonder she was apprehensive! But she wouldn't tell me that beforehand. It had been so important to her to be able to "make it" on that first pass. Yet, in spite of her determination, it had ended dismally.

Our second try was different. In the time lapse between, Mary had not only become more accustomed to the portable respirator, she had also accomplished the standing transfer. Now she could ride in the car just like everyone else. That would make everything so simple. I would just bring our own comfortable sedan. We could go out on the pass together—just we two!

This Saturday I parked in the same place and went through the same check-out procedures. We wheeled down the hall amid the same well wishes of other patients, still wanting to be reassuring and reinforcing to Mary.

This time I positioned her wheelchair alongside the open door of the sedan. With Mary still attached to her battery-powered, portable respirator by a long, vacuum-cleaner-type hose, I helped her transfer into the car. Then came the fearful moment when the hose had to be disconnected while the machine was placed inside the auto. I had gone over this procedure a hundred times in my mind so that I would be able to do it flawlessly in just moments. Now, would I be able to actually disengage the hose, move the heavy respirator and battery-pack into the back of the car, and then reattach the hose to Mary's body unit all in time! I began. In seconds I heard the first of what were to become familiar, heart-rending little cries from Mary. "Oh, Honey, hurry!" she said in a tiny voice. Fighting panic myself, I prayed for steadiness. I must not make a mistake! The respirator was in, it was connected to the battery-pack...the hose was connected... Mary was breathing in rhythm with the machine again.

In the first few minutes of the pass, I was already experiencing terrible emotional strain. I was sensing the awful drain of physical strength that emotional strain can place on the body. By the time I closed the door by Mary and walked around to the driver's side, my knees were shaking with an unfamiliar, rubbery unsteadiness. The last time I had felt that way had been years before as a member of a high school track team, and I had nearly collapsed from exhaustion after running a too-strenuous race. A few moments of emotional tension had similarly drained the strength from my limbs.

Fear can grip you in other ways, too. Sometimes, it begins inside you with a vague uneasiness that mounts finally to near panic. It may start with nothing more than a thought or observation. A paraplegic or a "quad" looks at himself and observes the wasted body and thinks, *I'm ugly and grotesque in appearance. Tiny shriveled-up arms and legs where once I had well-formed limbs. My chest isn't firm and well-proportioned any more. I'm now useless and helpless. I can't do any of the things I used to do!*

That observation begins a sequence of thought: *Who is going to want me? I'm not even a whole person any more! What if my wife (or husband) doesn't find me desirable now? Suppose she (he) begins to find others more attractive? How will I hold her love?* Fear begins to creep over the edge of consciousness in spite of the fact that the paralytic reminds himself that it is insane to think this way. Attitudes like that do strange things to behavior. They make you do bizarre things in grasping for assurance of love—assurance that otherwise would not be needed. But in spite of the possible consequences, those useless arms and legs are a grim and continuing suggestion to fear. Try as he might, he cannot shake that awful dread of being rejected and no longer wanted.

It is often reinforced by what we see in others. When Maxine, who lost her husband to a pretty hospital attendant, dissolved into tears of hopelessness and despair, the seeds of doubt and uncertainty were planted in Mary.

Millie's faithless husband took their child and disappeared forever from her life. As Mary watched what this heartbreak had done to Millie, she couldn't escape the eventual creeping, insidious doubt that overshadowed her own future.

It is mostly imagined and may be totally without basis in fact. Yet the fear is real! And you cannot control it. It makes little difference who you are. The fear of rejection is universal. Anyone who has ever felt inadequate, physically or emotionally, has known it. And who has not at some time felt inadequate? Every person who has lived on this planet has experienced at least one moment of the inner desolation borne of failing in relationship to others, and that moment has unbelievable power to trigger anxiety over possible future failure and isolation. This awful, inner aching repeats itself over and over again, feeding on itself, until a person experiences near panic with just the thought of closeness.

Mary told me of months of agony of soul after coming home from the hospital during which she wondered if she could keep me interested and in love with her. Early reassurances didn't really help much, either. On the occasion of our first pass from the hospital, Mary had voiced as best she could this fear, and efforts at reassurance carried little lasting comfort for her. *After all,* she thought, *it will be different when we are home and living together again. He means it all right now, but then it will change!* She had always been so active, so capable. Now she felt so useless! That uselessness was heightened as she watched our early housekeepers cooking favorite dishes for me, setting the table nicely, or listening to my well-meaning compliments for their efforts. She should be the one fixing creamed peas and new potatoes! *She* should be the one to think about spreading the pretty tablecloth to make the table "special" for dinner. *She* should be hearing all those delicious compliments. But she was . . . useless. It takes a lot of patient loving to convince one other-

47

wise. As a young man who knew and understood so little about feelings, about the awful phantoms of fear, about the deep unspoken yearnings of a lovely twenty-five-year-old girl, it was a wonder that any of those feelings were assuaged, any of those fears allayed, or any of those yearnings of love fulfilled. I had so much to learn about the feeling levels of life and about this wonderful, courageous girl to whom I was married.

Gradually, of course, the experiences of the passes grew more and more satisfying as we grew more confident. Surely, the trust that developed in Mary as she became more willing to fully commit her safety into my hands was of immeasurable value to our love and marriage. We couldn't have been aware of that at the time, but it even had an immediate effect on our lovemaking during those brief hours together.

As the time of the passes lengthened and made it feasible, we would rent a room in a motel nearby so that we could have privacy. At first, we felt a little strange, yet delightfully naughty in having sex together in a motel! It was a crazy, nonsensical feeling. For after all, we were married, weren't we? Yet there was a delightful stimulation to being alone in the motel room. We began to rediscover each other sexually after the long months of enforced restraint.

"You can't know how much I have needed you!" I tried to explain to her. That sounded all wrong. It sounded as though I had just needed her as a sex partner, and that wasn't what I meant at all! I was discovering that there had been a deep, unsatisfied longing within me all those months *just to be with her* in the privacy we could experience in that motel room. In this realization were the seeds of an understanding about the need a husband and wife have for each other that is infinitely more than sexual.

Achieving some sense of normalcy sexually, as well as every other way, took some deliberate effort after Mary came home from the hospital. She still wore the chest respirator (her "Tummick," as Karen called it) or used the positive pressure from the respirator to breathe. After having her "trach" closed surgically, that meant a hose held in her mouth. Neither of these is particularly romantic. In fact, they are downright awkward in the midst of sex! Yet, we learned to giggle at our clumsiness and gradually to pay little attention to the hoses.

One thing didn't resolve itself so easily, though. Somewhere early in Mary's illness I must have been struck forcefully by the vulnerability of her limbs to injury. At any rate, whenever I lay in bed beside her after that, I was super-sensitive to her paralyzed arms and hands. If I accidentally rolled over on one, I immediately felt a stab of fear lest I should break or in some way injure that hand.

Through the intervening years of observation and study as a pastoral counselor, I've found that a characteristic of sexual responsiveness is that it cannot remain at high levels of stimulation when fear or anxiety intrude. A woman who fears that a small child can overhear the sounds of lovemaking by Mother and Daddy will find herself strangely cold and unresponsive to her husband. (I always recommend to new parents that the baby be placed in a room by himself, not in the parents' bedroom. A couple should see to it that there is also a door between the rooms.) This same phenom-enon of cessation of sexual desire upon the intrusion of fear or anxiety overtook me each time I felt a hand or arm underneath my body's weight. It was like an instantaneous attack of impotency! An erection was impossible, obviously. So we continued lovemaking until I learned by experience that Mary just wasn't all that fragile! Yet even today, twenty years later, there are moments when I experience the same feelings. I must still push beyond them in order to continue making love to my wife.

Just the effort to get a good night's rest was not as simple as it would seem. How do you pull the blanket up over motionless shoulders and along both sides of a turtle-like body shell, and still have anything left for covering you? You don't! It's a little like trying to spread a round tablecloth over a rectangular table. It doesn't work. The shape is all wrong!

I realized the futility of this and eventually invested in twin beds, but these, in turn, produced their own problem of distance. Sleeping in twin beds, you lose the sense of closeness and physical stimulation. (The solution, however, was the delight of sexual encounter on the confining surface of a twin-sized bed!)

Other efforts to attain normalcy again were also often painful. I remember the hurdle we had to get over to return to routine in our ministry to youth. Mary and I had always been involved together with the youth of the churches where we had served. We even took our babies along to youth meetings. Now, Mary was hesitant to go along.

One night, our high school kids were scheduled to go miniature golfing. Mary announced that she wasn't going. "I'd be too much bother," she said. "You go along. You'll have more fun with the kids if I'm not in the way."

"I didn't get married to be alone," I replied. "I lived alone for the thirteen months you were in the hospital, and if I want to take you, you ought to be willing to go!" I could not have known how much that exchange would mean. Mary told me much later that I rescued her from becoming a

"I didn't get married to be alone..."

recluse by my insistence then and always that she be at my side "as usual."

Why young ministers try to stuff too many things into their daily schedules, I will never know, but I was no exception. It always seemed that I was a few minutes late to everything, and I hated to be late. Learning to pace ourselves for the extra routines of going about in the car took a little doing and practice. Traveling even across town with Mary and her equipment was like traveling with a baby. I had to learn to allow extra minutes to get the respirator and the chair into the car while superintending both Kenny and Karen.

One day, Mary and I were downtown shopping. We had only a limited time, as usual, and I was hurrying down the sidewalk, pushing the wheelchair. Suddenly, the small wheels at the front of the chair struck a break in the concrete. The chair stopped still. I grabbed for Mary to keep her from sliding out of the chair, but I missed. Down she went with a thump, sitting flat on the sidewalk! At first I was terrified, lest something was broken. As I carefully lifted her back into the chair and she assured me that nothing was amiss, the humor of the thing struck us both.

"I must have looked terribly feminine and attractive sitting there, spread-eagled on the cement," Mary said. The vision of that flashed back across my mind, and I dissolved in laughter. Years later, we still laugh about that incident, and Mary still gets a good deal of mileage out of shyly letting people know how careless I am about wheeling her in the chair!

Without a sense of humor, we scarcely could have survived. So many marriages that I work with in counseling have never known the wholesomeness and healing that can be experienced with a touch of humor. Even the most irritating and exasperating of life's little twists can take on an entirely different hue when we learn to laugh at ourselves and our ridiculous postures, "Oh, that God would give us the very smallest of gifts—to be able to see ourselves as others see us!"[1]

Before Mary could ever come home from the hospital, of course, arrangements had to be made for someone to care for her personal needs and those of the family. A housekeeper had to be found. Mary's lovely, patient mother helped us for the first week or so until we hired our first live-in housekeeper.

The selection of such a person seemed at first so simple to us. Just find someone who could cook and do housework and learn to do the few, specialized things that were required for Mary's care. Of course, we had developed a tolerance for those "few, specialized things" over a period of a year. Someone coming into our home for the first time was to be fairly overwhelmed by the magnitude of caring for our family of four, which included a totally dependent post-polio. How inconsiderate we must have been to those first durable, patient ladies who came to work for us!

We learned several things about having someone in one's home twenty-four hours of the day, every day. We discovered, for instance, some obvious things such as the variety of ways people do things. A simple task like cleaning the living room can be approached from an incredible number of ways. Some people dust and then vacuum; some vacuum and then dust. Some people "pick up" in the morning, some "pick up" at night, and some never "pick up" at all. Some people dust with furniture polish and burnish to a gleam; some dust only when you can write a name and address on the top of the dining table with your finger.

And how many ways are there to cook scrambled eggs? I was so naive that I thought everyone just whipped the eggs together in a bowl with a little milk and then poured them into the pan. (Would you believe that it was a long time before I realized that this wasn't even "scrambled eggs" at all?) After I saw at least four or five different ways of really *scrambling* eggs, I began to realize that all I knew about such things was a casual observation I had once made of my own mother in the kitchen preparing an omelet.

When Mary and I had observed the infinite manner of ways in which people have learned to do things in their own home situations, it began to penetrate our thinking that the same phenomenon influences marriages.

"You know, Honey," I said to Mary one day, "everyone who ever gets married seems to come to that marriage with a pre-established mindset about how things should be done. It is probably based upon the experiences they had in their own home as they grew up."

"Well, that's usually the only model they have to follow," Mary observed. "They will either decide as they grow up that the way things are done in their home makes for a happy home, and they therefore wish to emulate these practices when they establish their own home; or they decide that ways of doing things in their childhood home made for an unhappy experience, and they will do things in the opposite manner."

Dr. Paul Popenoe, former director of the American Institute of Family Relations, has written an engaging little book called *Marriage Before and After*.[2] In the chapter entitled "How to Adjust to Hasty Marriage," he talks about how every one of us starts in marriage with a ready-make idea of appropriate behavior. Everyone unconsciously sees himself in the role of a marriage partner. The young lady sees herself as what a good wife should be. The young man pictures himself as the ideal of a good husband—a picture that he has built up over the years from memories of his father, an admired uncle, or someone else.

So each comes to the marriage with a ready-made script for the prince and princess to act out. The young bride has a beautiful script for her prince to read. Since everyone knows just how a prince should behave, he will obviously read his script to perfection. The groom has also prepared a carefully written script for his princess. She will follow it to the letter, and they will live happily every after. Only neither reads the script the other has written! Usually, the first few years of marriage are given over to rewriting the script. The marriage that survives and becomes the fulfilling experience all couples dream about is the marriage in which this rewrite is done *together*.

But always a person is influenced in such everyday matters as cooking and housework (more than one knows) by one's mother. Unconsciously, people follow the same pattern later in life, and we are rarely aware of why we do things the way we do. By the time a woman takes a position in someone else's home as a housekeeping aide, patterns of doing things have been well established. And then just *try* to change them! It's not just a trite statement that we are creatures of habit. We humans are almost as bad as the dinosaurs who simply could not change their routines of life and so perished as the Ice Age crept upon them. Had they been more adaptive and moved south "for the winter," they would have survived, but they were creatures of habit—habits that would not, could not, change.

So much that damages a marriage comes from our bondage to habit. No one means to have routines so ingrained that change and adaptation are impossible. Yet, often in counseling troubled marriages I have found that good, seemingly sturdy marriages have been destroyed by an inability to adapt on the part of one or both of the marriage partners. Like the dinosaurs of old, *inflexibility* froze the marriage into *immobility*, and a marriage that isn't going anywhere is dead.

As Mary and I observed this important relationship between the ability and willingness to be adaptive and the survival and growth of marriage, we both resolved that whatever the cost, we would learn to adapt to each other! How we thank God that He showed us so many lessons about marriage from the everyday experiences of just learning how to make a household function in a new manner.

It wasn't too long after beginning this relearning process that we learned something about the value of solitude. Most young people in love are convinced they can scarcely survive if they are not in the physical presence of the beloved every waking moment. We began to suspect that there was a false-hood hidden away here somewhere after two things dawned upon us from our own experience. The first awareness came from sensing that having someone who was not "family" (no matter how gracious and thoughtful that person might be) in our home twenty-four hours of *every* day placed an unnatural strain upon behavior. We found that we could not demonstrate affection as freely as we desired. We were inhibited in expressing feelings of anger and frustration with someone else always about. In short, inhibition mounted! We were always guarding our words, our behavior. We couldn't really be ourselves at any time, even in our own home.

What happened then? Often the simple feelings of resentment that every husband and wife feel, and healthily ventilate in the course of wholesome confrontation, would build to unreasonable levels. Then in some moment in the car, away from home, when we should have been enjoying just being together, the lid would blow off all these repressed resentments, and we would have an unnecessary painful encounter.

It would often start over something totally unrelated. A careless driver who cut too sharply in front of us in traffic could make me explode, "That idiot! He almost caused us to have an accident. People like that have no business on the road!" A little later, still unnaturally angry at the careless driver, I might ask Mary for directions from the map held in her lap. If her response was not clear or not quick enough, I might snap at her with all the pent-up frustration of weeks before. How ridiculous! How bewildering to the one who is thus attacked. In such episodes, Mary didn't even know what had happened.

Probably the enforced caution in expressing emotion in our home was not the only factor leading to these encounters. When we married, I had some really strange ideas about marriage, especially about what the marriage of a minister should be like. Where I got them from is a mystery. There is not one minister in my entire background on either side of the family that I have ever met. It follows that I didn't get these ideas from any model I could have emulated. I suppose I just dreamed them up from imagining what a pious and holy life a minister must lead!

At any rate, I had the idea that in a minister's home there should never be any disagreements. Everything should always be calm and serene. Well, I tried that when we married. It worked for about three weeks. By that time, I had repressed so many feelings that I couldn't stand it. They began to surface even before the honeymoon had ended. Those emotions had to come out! I remember one way in which they emerged that proved disastrous. When I became angry over something, I often stormed out into the kitchen and began to do the dishes or clean up the kitchen. While I thought it was a capital idea to do something constructive to work off my anger, the message that came through to Mary was that I was voicing silent criticism of her housekeeping. Then, her anger mounted. Oh, woe! How we unwittingly punish each other!

Every human being alive probably has the need to be alone at some time. Solitude is somehow one of the ingredients of sanity. We learned this about ourselves as persons, too. It begins to creep over you like a pall, silently and insidiously, that awareness that you are always under observation. You never are really *alone*. There is not one single moment you can withdraw from everyone. Something inside you cries out for solitude!

No wonder the Bible records that often Jesus withdrew from the crowds that would press in upon Him, and even from His own inner circle of disciples, to seek the solitude of a night alone in prayer. If our Lord required such aloneness, how much more should we expect the need of solitude. Mary and I found that to be very real in our home.

Mary began to design moments of solitude. She would wheel her chair into a bedroom where she could be alone. I often found her quietly sitting in a semi-darkened room when I came home from work. At first, I thought that something unpleasant had happened during the day. Gradually, I learned that she was just doing what I had greater opportunity to do in being outside the home—seeking solitude. It was often during these moments of aloneness that she found opportunity to deal with her fears and feelings. She and God would talk them over. Married to a typical male who sensed very little about those feelings, she had to talk about them to someone, and God was such a good listener. I had begun my school of prayer in the hours driving back and forth to the hospital. Mary continued now what had begun for her in lonely, midnight hours in drab, antiseptic isolation rooms. She now deliberately sought time alone—time that she could, by her own choice, share with Jesus. We were gradually learning about the meaning of solitude, of meditation, and of oneness with our loving God.

"and the prayer of faith..."

I think it was Will Rogers who said that nobody is funnier than people. How true! Certainly, the unbelievable variety of persons who have lived and worked in our home confirms it. More than a hundred different housekeepers have come and gone in twenty-two years. Many have left us with laughable memories. Some have departed leaving us feeling sad—for them. A few have stolen a piece of our hearts. All have instructed us about human nature. What a rich study that is.

For some time, I struggled to write a chapter about the fascinating experiences we have had with housekeepers. So much of our understanding of human nature has come from these encounters. The chapter was to have been light and airy and filled with delightful personal glimpses into life shared with these women in our home.

There were so many ludicrous things we remembered. I thought of the lady, for instance, who had made sandwiches for lunch one day using leftover pancake batter as sandwich spread. Those were sandwiches that would *really* stick to your ribs! On another occasion, we had a lady who seemed to lack some ability to organize her time. Everything was going well during our first week together until I began to notice an absence of shirts in my closet. In fact, I didn't have a single one left to wear to work that day. When I asked the housekeeper if she could iron one for me, I was startled to see her walk into the living room. She went directly to the couch against the wall and extracted a shirt from behind the couch.

"What are my shirts doing behind the couch?" I asked in stunned amazement.

"That's where I always keep the ironing till I get to it," she replied, without even batting an eye.

Later, we employed a lady who was much better about the ironing but who had a problem with some kinds of cleaning. I was in the hospital for surgery at the time, so we felt especially fortunate to have someone at home to take care of Mary. As so often happens when there isn't a man at home to fix it, the toilet in the bathroom stopped up and overflowed. This lady grudgingly cleaned up the mess but not without some evidence of distaste. Only hours later the plumbing once again failed. This time she surveyed the scene in the flooded bathroom and remarked with finality, "*Well, I'm* not going to clean it up! After all, I *did* that once!"

Sometimes, younger girls in their later teen years would interview for the job. Though it usually proved too confining for an eighteen or nineteen-year-old, occasionally one would attempt the regimen. These had somewhat unorthodox means of terminating if they wished to leave. All sorts of excuses appeared as reasons. One manufactured from thin air a marriage with a now-suddenly-hospitalized husband she had to go visit. Another got a "telegram" from "back home."

Simply telling us that they wanted to quit seemed just too much to face. One left a note on the dresser and crawled out through the window with her suitcases!

I remember the lovely, big, black lady who was such a phenomenal cook. Her voluminous size offered no handicap to her culinary skill. How fortunate we had felt to have her, until the third or fourth evening when she failed to emerge from her room about suppertime. Thinking she might have fallen asleep on this quiet, winter evening, I gently knocked at her door. Then, I knocked a little louder. Finally, I opened the door and peered into the blackness inside. No sign of anyone at all! I then heard a voice coming brokenly out of the inky blackness, "Have yewr...big boy...come heah...ah'll pay him...to fix suppa". Looking intently into the darkened room, I could finally make out the outline of the bed standing some distance from the wall. The lady had imbibed too much during the afternoon and had rolled off the bed. In her inebriated state she had become stuck between the bed and the wall. She couldn't budge her two hundred pounds, and I couldn't even see her black countenance in the inky blackness of the room.

Obviously, not all the experiences we had with housekeepers were funny. The entire range of human emotions was tied to association with one or another of these persons. Humorous memories keep fading into other kinds of memories. Some of the people I remember were girls and women who had filled our hearts with warmth. One of these was Sudie.

We had already had a half-dozen housekeepers come and go when Sudie came to help out. We were still in San

Bernardino, and Sudie was in the youth department of the church there. She was fourteen at the time. Her first day during that summer was really memorable.

That Saturday morning she asked Mary, "What do you people like to eat for breakfast?" I have rather weird tastes which Mary has always accommodated, so she suggested to Sudie that she fix creamed tuna on toast. The whole idea of such a revolting thing for breakfast just about did Sudie in, to say nothing of the fact that she didn't have the vaguest idea of how to prepare such a gastronomical oddity. The remainder of the day went fairly well until about 5:30 that afternoon. Then Dave called.

Now Dave was the handsome, dark-haired son of Dr. Miles Dawson, our pastor. Dave was an accomplished actor, organist, and composer—all at age sixteen! What a dream he was, and he called Sudie for a date that night.

What should I do? she thought. *I'll just die if I can't go out with Dave. This is the first time he's ever asked me for a date, and if I say no, he may never ask me again! But I can't leave my job on the first day! I'll just have to ask Mary what to do.* So she told Dave to call her back in a little while because she would have to ask Mary. Of course, Mary encouraged her to go, and she made emergency arrangements for someone to stay with her.

Sudie has never forgotten that first date. Out of that beginning has grown one of the most cherished relationships of our life. Sue (she uses a more grown-up name now) is still among our dearest and closest friends. We have followed her training and career as a psychiatric social worker with pride, tears, and prayers.

Another woman who brings back unusual memories of love and kindness is Mrs. Clara Hull. Clara was seventy-nine when she first came to work for us. Imagine! She was about as big as a minute, yet because she knew how to pace herself carefully through the day, she could still carry out the tasks of caring for our family of four.

She came into our lives at an especially appropriate time. Mary had lost her mother just a couple of months before. Mrs. Hull's daughter had died only a short time earlier. They needed each other.

What a wise woman Clara was. She had lived a full life in her seventy-nine years. She had even held jobs with some of the country's leading newspapers as one of the nation's first lady typesetters. All of her experience and wisdom of years were shared with Mary in a quiet, unassuming manner. When we were upset about the children, she would say to Mary, "Now dear, remember, somebody had to teach you..."

She was a perfect example of the Apostle Paul's admonition that the "older women...train the younger" (Titus 2:3–4, RSV). A year ago, it was a personal honor to hold her memorial service. She had met death in an auto accident while riding to work at the Pacific State Hospital where she was employed in the Grandmother Program. She was almost ninety-three!

Without doubt the most remarkable housekeeper we have met has to be Mrs. "C" (that's short for Clendaniels). She must be some sort of an angel in disguise. For seventeen years, she has come every Monday and Tuesday, allowing the live-in person (when we have had one) two days off each week. She has done washing and ironing, taken Mary shopping, loaned us grocery money when we were broke, come to fill in for emergencies when other housekeepers left unexpectedly, and all the while she has worked five days a week at her other job to raise her family by herself!

We have come to love her as part of our own family. Because we couldn't have survived without her, there is no limit to our admiration and love for this unusual lady. Now, during her retirement years, it has been especially delightful to have her travel with us on vacations. God must have a reward of enormous magnitude awaiting this saint in slippers!

Somehow, as I have remembered these things and a thousand others, the chapter that I *wanted* to write just wouldn't take shape. The writing wouldn't come. I began to wonder if the plan for the chapter was a mistake. *Perhaps, God doesn't even want me to write this chapter at all,* I began to muse. As I prayed, I felt no inner peace about the chapter development.

After three months of almost futile attempts to write it, I wrote to our dear friends, Dick and Joyce Landorf. I thought Joyce would be able to advise me. She's written so many excellent, helpful books, and she gave so much time and counsel to me when I began writing. "I'm stuck," I wrote her. "I can't get this chapter together. I have bits and pieces, but nothing comes together. Please pray with me about it. Maybe God doesn't want me even to write this chapter at all. I just don't know."

A couple of weeks later, I had occasion to call Joyce about wedding arrangements for her lovely daughter Laurie.

At the end of that conversation, I mentioned my continued frustration over the chapter. Joyce asked, "What chapter is it you're having trouble with?"

"The one about the housekeepers—the one I wanted to make funny and light," I answered.

"When you wrote me a couple of weeks ago I didn't even know what chapter you were having trouble with," Joyce continued, "so I prayed that God would help me to be wise in answering you. Keith, ever since you first shared the outline of this book with me, I've been concerned that the approach for that chapter wasn't correct. Making it light and airy just isn't right!"

"What do you mean, Joyce? The rest of the book gets pretty heavy in spots. Shouldn't there be some humor somewhere?"

"Keith, what's the real lesson behind those twenty-two years of housekeepers coming and going? Do you see what this is really all about? Dick and I have prayed *for years* that God would send you someone who would love you two, and who would take the job as housekeeper as a real ministry to you and Mary. And that would free you up in your own personal ministry to others. We've been frustrated again and again. We couldn't understand why God didn't do it. You and Mary, too, have agonized in prayer over this thing through the long years. But that's exactly what this is all about—how you and Mary have coped with unanswered prayer, how you've handled it. Don't you see? You've got to write about that! Of course, you've handled it in your own life with a sense of humor— you've seen all the funny things along the way. But what's the real answer you've learned over the years? That's what this chapter should be about! There are so many dear Christians all over the country who need to read what you can write about this. Use humor if you want, but this chapter will be powerful if you can tell people how to cope with this experience—if you can explain this whole thing of unanswered prayer."

I sat somewhat stunned as I listened to Joyce on the telephone. I *knew* that she had put her finger right on the key issue. God had spoken through her directly to me! Without a doubt housekeepers have, through the years, been the greatest single unanswered prayer in our lives. They still are today! Because my work takes me out of the house several nights a week, and because Mary is totally dependent upon someone's assistance twenty-four hours of every day, there's nothing funny or light about it at all. No wonder I had been having a tough time getting this chapter "off the ground." I had been working entirely in the wrong direction.

As I thought about our conversation, I remembered the many times that as a minister I had also heard the cry, "How come God doesn't answer my prayer for...?" and then the person voices any one of hundreds of valid requests that have been presented to the heavenly Father. "I have prayed earnestly for this for years, and God hasn't answered. What's the trouble? Is it that my faith is too weak?"

I would now answer that it may have nothing at all to do with your faith, or lack of it. Well-meaning people may have told you that if you just "have enough faith" you will receive your every request, and they have pointed automatically to Jesus' own words in the New Testament: "'If ye have faith as a grain of mustard seed, ye shall say unto this mountain, Remove hence to yonder place; and it shall remove; and nothing shall be impossible unto you'" (Matthew 17:20). Or they may choose His words in Mark 9:23: "'If thou canst believe, all things are possible to him that believeth.'"

That sounds so easy! What more is there than to just "have faith" and to believe? "But then," you argue in your heart, "why don't I see the results of my prayers? I must lack faith!"

Let me ask you, how *much* faith is necessary to have prayers answered? And what is the *source* of that faith?

The words of Jesus seem to answer the first part of that question. It doesn't take much, but where do we go for the answer to the second part?

The Apostle Paul teaches a great deal about faith. One of the things he says about faith is that it is a gift from the Holy Spirit. In his first letter to the church at Corinth, he is speaking to them about the gifts that the Holy Spirit gives to the Church. He says in 12:9, "To another [He gives] faith by the same Spirit." Now, as faith is given only by the Spirit "to every man severally as he wills" (1 Corinthians 12:11), if answers to prayer depended only upon how much faith we had, then we could infer from that kind of thinking that in some cases the Holy Spirit doesn't give enough faith to some for their prayers to be answered. How absurd! Even cruel! No, thank heaven, God doesn't play games like that!

If faith, only as much as a grain of mustard seed, is all that is needed to realize the astonishing kinds of things Jesus referred to, then it doesn't require much faith to have great

> God is big!...
> God is love! ...
> God is wise!

things happen. Could it be, then, that the *amount* of faith has little to do with the matter at all? Could it be rather that even the *tiniest* faith can be the vehicle through which the *power of God* flows at His discretion and choice?

Mary and I have come to terms with some shattering ideas about God over the years. One of those is that *God is big!* Another is that *God is love!* Still another is that *God is wise!* God is bigger than I am, and He is bigger than my circumstances are. God is wiser than my puny efforts to solve my problems and control my circumstances, and God is far too loving to do everything for me I want Him to do. He's also far too kind to allow me to see the future. I've often wanted to. I guess everyone has at some time or another, but what a disaster that would make of our nervous systems! Seeing tomorrow's trauma today would force us all into the worst kind of dread and anxiety. No wonder Jesus once said, "'Take...no thought for the morrow...Sufficient unto the day is the evil thereof.'" (Matthew 6:34)

One morning in staff prayer at the church, Dave Zehring, our minister to high schoolers, prayed, "Father, I'm thankful that You see the end from the beginning. It blows my mind, God, that right now *You* are seeing the end of my life—and the beginning—all at the same time! I can't handle that kind of greatness, Father, but I thank You for it!"

I can't either! But it is wonderful to be able to catch hold of that idea about God in any way that works for you in everyday life. Jesus' teaching about not being anxious about *anything* seems nice to us, but a little unworkable. Actually, we tend to think that those words were probably meant for more spiritual folks than we are. We've got far too much "anxiety material" to worry over.

What our Lord may have been trying to tell us is that a loving, wise, big God already has it all worked out. Oh, it doesn't make too much sense from where we're sitting, but He's got a plan all right!

As you read this, you may be asking, "What are you driving at, Keith? Are you going to tell me that I just have to *trust* God when my prayer is unanswered?" I can hear you saying to me, "That's about as much help as telling me I have to have more faith!"

So I have to tell you, no, that's not what I want to say to you at all. That's not what we've learned, Mary and I, over these twenty-two years. What we have learned is that we don't have to feel "unspiritual" (and thus guilty) for not understanding, for not even *liking*, our circumstances sometimes. We don't have to feel like a spiritual pauper when we don't get "Instant Answering Service" from God. We don't have to sit in sackcloth and ashes every time our prayers are not immediately fulfilled because we've learned that God loves us. And He shows that love in an incredible kind of acceptance of us.

During the frequent times we are without a housekeeper, things can get rather hectic around our house. Unless I stick to a fairly rigid schedule in the mornings, for instance, we just can't seem to make it, no matter how early I get up and begin.

71

So I have this little plan. I struggle out of bed about thirty to forty minutes before I intend to help Mary up. I grope my way into the bathroom to shower and shave. This helps me achieve some degree of humanness again, and then I go to the kitchen to fix our breakfast. While the coffee is perking, I go back to help Mary from bed into the bathroom. While she's there; I go back into the bedroom, make the beds, and put away her respirator and shell. Next, out to the kitchen we go for breakfast. Afterward, the dishes get rinsed and stacked in the dishwasher. Finally, I'm ready to take Mary back to the bathroom to bathe and dress her. Then, I put on my tie and coat, and we're off to take her to someone's home for the day. It's a great schedule. If I keep on it, we can do beautifully.

But do you know what? Sometimes, I *hate* that schedule! Sometimes, I get fed up with the routine.

But something happens somewhere in the middle of my whispered conversation with God while I'm straightening the bedspread. I'm muttering to Him about how grim this all is—and how unfair I think it is that we don't have a housekeeper—and He always lets me know He still accepts me, even with my complaining. He sort-of smiles and says, "Sure, I know, you're a little bent out of shape this morning, and you just *want* to feel crummy for a while. That's okay. I can handle that all right. Go ahead and get it out of your system and then let's get on with the day." (At least, I always *feel* like He's smiling when He says it.) And then sometimes I want to burst right out laughing because this is all so comical. To think that I'm talking this way to God, and He still accepts me.

That helps me know that obedience isn't always liking my situation, but it is a practical way of trusting Him in the middle of it. Because I've learned that even the routine isn't forever. Eventually, another housekeeper will come along. Meanwhile, God is not disturbed one bit by my ups and downs. He just keeps trying to teach me not to take myself and my circumstances too seriously.

Probably, one of the best things that has come out of twenty-two years of praying for a housekeeper has been learning how to ask for help from people. For some folks that seems to come easily. For me, it was really hard. Even Mary struggled at first in asking young women of the church to help us during the in-between-housekeeper times.

Eventually, though, we realized that something really beautiful was happening. These women and their husbands were becoming some of our most cherished friends. We were increasing in our love for them as they gave of themselves to us. They, in turn, were discovering the richness and satisfaction that comes from investing themselves in others. Can you believe that some have even *thanked us* for what it did for them? They needed the opportunity to serve, to "bear one another's burden." We needed to learn how to receive gracefully. We all grew!

I guess that's part of the way we've learned to cope with unanswered prayer—by seeing the growth that comes to us in tough situations. In realizing that God uses these distasteful experiences as the raw material from which He fashions growth in us, we have found it easier. Not that we have always liked the fact that it seems to be only difficulty that produces growth. I wish there were some other way to make it happen! Probably, even the oyster isn't *overjoyed* by the grain of sand that gets lodged inside his shell, yet he grows a pearl out of his discomfort. God has a way of doing that in us, and He does it a little at a time—gradually, like making a pearl.

In early years, we were seldom without a housekeeper. Our children were small, and we were less sure of either ourselves or our love for each other. Gradually, as we became more secure in our mutual love, and the children grew enough to be more help than helped. The periods when we were without housekeeping help became more frequent and longer in duration. God tailored the stress to our levels of endurance. This reminds me a little of the verse in 1 Corinthians 10:13: "No temptation [trial] has overtaken you that is not common to man. God is faithful, and he will not let you be tempted [tried] beyond your strength, but with the temptation will also provide the way of escape, that you may be able to endure it (RSV)."

I don't know much about your special trial in life. Maybe you were in Vietnam and had half your body shot away by mortar fire. Maybe, you've been feeling that life came to a screeching halt for you that day and that marriage and a family and all that stuff you used to dream about could never be a reality for you now. Or maybe you've just lost your marriage partner in a tragic, painful divorce. You couldn't believe it was happening to you when he came home and told you there was someone else. The pain you've felt since that day has been indescribable.

Maybe your baby was born just a few days ago, and you just found out he has a terrible disease. He will never live a normal life. Your heart is broken with sorrow, and you don't know if you can really face the endless tomorrows of caring for him.

No, I don't know your special trial. If I did, I don't know that I could carry what you are called to bear! I only know God makes us strong enough for our own special trials. In the process of praying to seek His strength and the waiting that's

...God makes us strong enough for our own special trials.

sometimes necessary, you get to know Him very well.

That's the other thing that has enabled us to cope with unanswered prayer. We've really gotten to know God a whole lot better! Everything we have found out about Him has confirmed His incredible love for us. I really wonder, how many people *feel* as deeply loved by God as Mary and I?

Getting to know Him in this way has meant sharing my muttering, grumbling, complaints and knowing He doesn't mind letting me be my own, nasty self at that point. It has meant hurling my demands at God sometimes in frustration and anger and seeing in the midst of the onslaught how idiotic I look trying to run the universe! It's meant sometimes laughing with God over the utter absurdity of our situation, and developing a sense of humor that refuses to take it all too seriously.

But most of all, it's meant a quiet kind of trust that's built between friends—God and me. Without that sense of quiet certitude produced by our friendship, the whole thing would have "gone down the drain" a long time ago. (When friends really trust each other, one doesn't have to have explanations for every curious turn of events. Somehow, each knows the eventual explanation will be forthcoming, and when it does, it will be sufficient.)

There's another curious thing about this matter of "unanswered" prayer. Every one is given God's strictest attention, and each is answered. Our difficulty with this is that there is such a variety of answers that He gives, we don't always understand some of them. The "yes" answers we handle quite well. God is giving us exactly what we prayed for, and we are extremely well pleased with God and ourselves.

When God says no, we have a little more trouble with that. At this point, we're completely sure that God hasn't heard us well and, thus, doesn't fully comprehend the seriousness of our particular situation, or we begin to feel that Jesus' parable about the woman who kept hounding the judge about her case until he answered was written specifically for us. We believe, therefore, that we should barrage the gates of heaven with our prayers until God changes His mind (Yet to think that we change the mind of God in any way is not only ludicrous beyond description but downright belittling to God).

Sometimes, we must accept the "no" answer from God with the same simple trust of a child accepting "no" from his daddy. The five-year-old doesn't pretend to understand. Indeed, he probably cannot. The issues are too complex and too far beyond his experience to comprehend, yet it simply does not occur to him that his daddy doesn't really love him or that he doesn't really care. It doesn't matter to the five-year-old that he doesn't understand! To be sure, he will have his feelings hurt by a negative response from his daddy, but that's not a lack of faith or trust in daddy. He will get over his little pout, and at no time does he *doubt* his daddy!

With so many suggestions in the Bible about our becoming as little children in this matter of faith, it's strange that we feel it is too demeaning for us to demonstrate that kind of uncomplicated, simple, direct believing! When God says to us, "No, not now. Later!" that's even harder to handle. Joyce Landorf speaks frequently in her seminars for women around the country about the "waiting room" of life. Every one of us can think of times when it seemed God had just placed our request on "hold," and we were just sitting and waiting. Waiting rooms aren't much fun. They are trying, enervating, debilitating experiences. During those six hours at the emergency waiting room when Mary first became ill, I didn't find anything particularly pleasant about the situation. It was sheer desperation. Many of our waiting rooms in life are like that.

When our daughter Karen was in ninth grade, she met a good-looking young boy at Palomares Junior High School. Although she was too young to date, they began seeing a lot of each other. It grew really serious. So serious, in fact, that she dated this young man all the way through high school. She was his steady girlfriend for four whole years. Mary and I wanted her to date other boys, but Karen was committed to this one. We liked him well enough, but we suspected he would not be well-suited to become a lifelong partner for Karen. He was a "professing" Christian but certainly not a serious and growing one. Somewhere along about Karen's sophomore year in high school, we began to pray, "Lord, you know we like this boy all right. He's just not the right one for Karen. Can't you help her see that too?"

It seemed that God just put that request on "hold." Nothing happened. Absolutely nothing. Karen went on to her junior year, and her senior year, and it seemed that she might actually marry this young man after a year or two at college. Our efforts to include him in family gatherings and vacations didn't have any of the intended effect to show that he just didn't fit into our family lifestyle. All this time—for four years—while Mary and I were experiencing quiet desperation over this, God had kept absolutely still. He hadn't said yes, no, or maybe. We were in a holding pattern—a waiting room.

When Karen went away to Westmont College, we helped her move her things to the dorm that first semester. Everything went pretty well for "Dear Old Dad" until it was finally time for us to drive away and leave her there all alone. I looked at Karen and just couldn't stand it. I took her in my arms, and we clung to each other for a long time. I suspect that somewhere deep inside of me I was giving her up to more than just college life away from home for four years. Probably, I was also giving her up to a young man that I didn't really feel was God's choice for her life. It was a hard moment. We both cried softly as we held each other.

The waiting room continued only until about midyear. As Karen was among the stimulating, spiritually growing students at Westmont, somehow interest in her boyfriend diminished. God had already arranged for someone else to come on the scene a little later. When Scott Jacobs stepped on stage, it was amazing how quickly the curtain came down on the former scene. In only a matter of weeks this rollicking, mischievous, delightful young man had completely captured Karen's heart! When Scott asked for Karen's hand in marriage during her senior year at college, Mary and I couldn't have been more glad and excited. Our waiting room was over.

All that came to Mary and to me as a result of the waiting is hard to measure. We have a son-in-law who is everything any father and mother could want for their daughter. We have seen the hand of God at work in their two lives together in ways that have caused our spirits to soar. We have watched Scott skillfully assume his spiritual leadership in their home and seen how this has brought deep, inner satisfaction, stability and maturity to Karen. The waiting rooms are always designed for multiple, unexpected blessings like that.

At one point in his amazing ministry, the Apostle Paul entered his own special waiting room. Oh, it wasn't about housekeepers or daughters who are dating the wrong boys or things like that, but it was a time of waiting, nonetheless. He was on his way through Asia Minor to a region called Bithynia. In Acts 16, we can read the narrative of how he was frustrated by God in carrying out his purpose to go there. The biblical account says, "They headed north for the province of Bithynia, but again the Spirit of Jesus said no. So instead they went on through Mysia province to the city of Troas" (Acts 16:7–8, TLB).

The fascinating thing about this restraint God placed upon the apostle was the eventual outcome of this change of direction. When Paul reached the city of Troas, he had to simply wait. He didn't know where to go next. He was completely frustrated and bewildered by being hemmed in and waiting there before God's Spirit. Then, he had a vision from God of a man over in Northern Greece (the province of Macedonia) calling for him to come over the Aegean Sea and help him. Actually, Paul's response to the Macedonian call was the first introduction of the Gospel to Europe and the Western world. The unexpected outcome of Paul's waiting room at Troas was that you and I would have an opportunity to hear about God's love demonstrated in Jesus Christ His Son!

Sometimes, God says yes to our prayers. Sometimes, He answers no. Sometimes, He makes us wait a little while, and sometimes He answers in such an unexpected and startling way that we often fail to even recognize which prayer is being answered.

When I prayed as a young minister, "Lord, help me to become a better minister, husband, and father," I had no idea God would do it by limiting our housekeeper help! He almost missed me altogether with that one. It was a while before I got the right answer hooked up with the right request. Only God could have thought up an answer like that, yet out of our frustration and tears over this unending problem, I *have* become a better minister. I am more empathetic now to others' struggles. I *have* become a better husband. I have grown closer to Mary as I have found it necessary to arrange my schedule to include her, often several times a week. Perhaps, I would not have been otherwise smart enough to spend that much time with my wife. Though I did not recognize this to be an answer to the earlier prayer, God was busy responding in His typical wise and loving way.

The other day, a man sat in my office discussing a problem of his and said, "I'm tired of fooling around with this problem. I want to get it resolved!" It occurred to me that some problems are perhaps never fully

"My grace is sufficient for thee."

resolved. How do you "resolve" multiple sclerosis? Or blindness? Or amputation of a limb? Or loss of a loved one in death? There's just no way to adequately resolve such matters. Each presents its *continued sense* of loss, handicap, or perplexity. Each haunts us with its special brand of fear. We must live with these and deal with them each day of our lives as best we can.

As I mentioned earlier, even the great Apostle Paul understood something of the frustration that has gripped every one of us victimized by some dreaded disease or misfortune in life. He spoke of his great desire to rid himself of a "thorn in the flesh" in writing to the Corinthian Church (2 Corinthians 12:7–9) yet was given no "resolution" to the problem. God answered by saying, "My grace is sufficient for thee: for my strength is made perfect in weakness."

Paul could have reasoned like most of us. He might have been tempted to say to God, "Now look, God, I know you can supply grace to *endure* this thing, but I could be so much more effective and efficient in ministry without this handicap. After all, I don't *need* this thing always slowing me down in my travels all over the Mediterranean!" We often reason thus with God, and we miss the real issue behind it all.

81

NOT A SOMETIMES LOVE

Have you ever looked at the writings of the Apostle Paul as they represent different periods of his life? For example, have you noted how different his letters to Timothy are from his letter to the church at Galatia? In the former, there is a tenderness that is hard to discover in earlier letters. What caused Paul to mellow and become more tolerant in later life? Why did he see John Mark with a totally different view in later years? How was it that even in writing about those who had fallen into sin in the church, the Apostle seemed more tender and tolerant in later epistles? Was it only advancing age? He certainly was no less lucid or logical in thought. Could it have been rather that in living through the years with his own unresolved problem Paul began to understand more clearly that life is not always "either/or" or "black and white"? Sometimes, it is "both/and" with degrees of grey in between. That is not compromise with life; it is the simple wisdom that accepts what cannot be changed. It would seem that we often do a great disservice to our children by teaching them, either by word or deed, that everything in life which is not satisfactory by our personal standards can be, and even ought to be, changed. Perhaps, that just isn't true. Perhaps, there are things in life that bring the greater good to us simply by their stubbornness and resistance to change.

A child often wishes to change the whole climate of discipline in his home. If he could have his way, all restraint would be immediately abolished. At least for the present, he would have no rules, no regulations. However, we know from a more experienced vantage point in life that such a thing would not only be foolhardy it might even lead to personal danger or disaster for the child. The rules are better than the desired change. Even the irritation of restraint has its place in the development of that which we call self-control.

In adult life, we make the same mistakes in value judgments. Women who have become pregnant in their later years have often confided to me these "accidental" pregnancies had initially caused them great consternation and distress, yet the resulting baby had brought each mother greater satisfaction and fulfillment than any earlier children she had borne.

In the entry hall of our home hangs a beautiful plaque given to us by our son Kenneth and his lovely wife Kim. The plaque carries the oft-quoted words of St. Francis of Assisi: "Lord, grant me the serenity to accept the things I cannot change; courage to change the things I can; and wisdom to know the difference."

Indeed, some things in life cannot be changed. They will *never* be "resolved." But do they need to be?

Most of the things that we want changed in life are things that affect our comfort or convenience—not our destiny. They are things God uses most effectively to develop in us a "patience of life"—that beautiful, winsome quality that one often sees in persons who have endured great suffering. They have known the crucible of pain, the agony of struggle, the tear-drenched distress of continued frustration. They have grown a great "patience of life." Somehow, God has helped them now to be at peace with the struggle, to be able to smile at the distress of frustration, and to come out of those periods of pain refined, tenderized, empathetic to *all* the hurts of the world around them.

The patience of life they have grown is not a kind of resigned, dispirited capitulation to life. Rather, one senses it is a deep, strong, gentle wisdom that sees life as it really is and has learned to meet it and deal with it in terms that are uniquely poised and balanced. The psalmist describes that person in Psalm 112:6–8:

> Such a man will not be overthrown by evil circumstances. God's constant care of him will make a deep impression on all who see it. He does not fear bad news, nor live in dread of what may happen. For he is settled in his mind that Jehovah will take care of him. That is why he is not afraid, but can calmly face his foes (TLB).

Unanswered prayer? No such thing! God's ways of answering are just often beyond our understanding, that's all! He's making us into the people He has always dreamed we might become, and in His wisdom, He's using even the distasteful touches of life as some of the materials.

And you know...we *still* don't have a housekeeper!

love and intimacy

Most young couples in the early years of marriage comprehend little of the concept of true intimacy. Sex is the immediate thought of many when intimacy is mentioned. Dr. Howard Clinebell's book *The Intimate Marriage* enlarges the concept to its proper proportions. Those proportions encompass so much more than sexual intercourse alone:

> *Intimacy is an art with as many expressions as there are artists to express it. It is often expressed in the sharing of thoughts and ideas and feelings. It is expressed in shared joys and sorrows, in respect for the deepest needs of the other person, and in the struggle to understand him. Intimacy does not suggest a saccharine sentimentalism; it can be expressed in constructive conflict which is the growing edge of a relationship. Intimacy is not a constant, but is expressed in varying degrees in the ebb and flow of day-in, day-out living. And intimacy is never a once-and-for-all achievement but must be nurtured throughout marriage; with this care, it grows and changes with the stages and seasons of marriage.*[3]

Mary and I needed to learn about these things like most other young couples. Perhaps "our" handicap served to help us in some ways. Certainly, intimacy is fostered by the spirit

> *Each victory was something we reached together.*

of cooperation. While it may be happening unconsciously, you learn about this in order to survive.

Can you imagine how clumsy a quadriplegic feels? The "spork" was only one of the devices we learned to master together. Yes, that's right—together! It wasn't just a frustrated Mary attempting again and again to pinch together thumb and forefinger hard enough to hold a pen. It wasn't only she who was so agonizingly forming letters and learning to write all over again. It wasn't just she who was so painfully tired, exercising endlessly to build strength in those emaciated muscles. No—there was always another. Another who was standing on the sidelines wanting *desperately* to help, crying out inside to relieve the awful tiredness of ceaselessly trying and failing, reaching and missing, grasping and spilling. Another who wanted so often just to lend a helping hand, but who by sheer determination must refrain, who must bite his lip, fight back the tears and let her spill the soup, struggle and fail, vent frustration, and finally...succeed! What emotional cost there is to both in that success, but oh, what a sense of intimacy and of oneness! We somehow knew each victory was something we reached together. Our efforts were on different sides of the lap board, but we did it together, Mary and me. She would look up finally from some little success with her eyes glistening through her tears, to meet my eyes filled and brimming over as I cried shamelessly in pride of the accomplishment. There was oneness. There was intimacy on a deep level that grew from our shared struggles.

Intimacy also grows from interdependence, but learning this lesson is difficult at very best. Marriage counselors often say that we marry the kind of person we need. That is, we unconsciously seek out the kind of person who will complement our own personality. For example, they point out to us how frequently we have observed some people who can't handle money at all—who let it run through their fingers like so much water—marry others who are "tighter than the bark on a tree." "Day" persons marry "night" persons and so on. Even when marriages fail and mates seek new partners, they still tend to seek out the same kind of person in the second attempt at marriage. Ironically, those qualities that draw us together before marriage are often the very ones that irritate us so during marriage! That's partly why learning the attitude or spirit of interdependence isn't easy.

Mary is a wonderfully feminine person. When she was a little girl, I'm told she was something of a tomboy. When we met during our college days, she was still very active and alive, completely a woman—absolutely feminine. Being really feminine has little to do with frills and laces, but it has a great deal to do with a way of perceiving and handling life. Women just do that differently from men.

We had a hard time understanding this at first. Conversations concerning some mutual problem to be solved were a good example. One day, Mary succeeded in getting me to sit down long enough to really talk about a problem involving Karen. By this time, Karen was growing into the troubled teen years. She was typical of many teenagers who become defiant and difficult to live with for a while. Was this just a "phase" that we could expect to pass, or were we doing something wrong as parents that caused her misbehavior?

"Honey, I think we may be failing in our responsibility to her," Mary said.

"Probably nothing that serious," I countered. "She'll grow out of this in a little while. It's just a phase."

"No, I don't feel you're being serious enough about this. She's getting worse instead of better. We've got to find out what's causing her to be like this."

The conversation didn't really go anywhere because we were perceiving the problem from two entirely different points of view and unable to see that simple fact. Instead, we eventually became annoyed with each other for not being more "perceptive" about the problem. Mary was looking at the problem from a typically feminine point of view, a feeling-level perception, while I was taking the masculine view of looking at the facts and going straight to the solution.

On another occasion, Mary was describing her frustration over one of the housekeepers. "She moves so slowly it drives me up the wall! We don't get anything done the whole morning. By the time the breakfast dishes are done and she bathes and dresses me, it's time to fix lunch!"

"Well, maybe you'll just have to prod her more," I suggested. "Why not tell her that you only have ten minutes for this and...?" About this time Mary became hurt and angry with me. But what had I done? I thought we were on the same side, and suddenly, I found I was on the opposing team. All I had done was attempt to solve the problem, but that was precisely what was wrong. Mary didn't need, or even want, my solution at that moment. (It turned out later that she already knew what she was going to do about it.) What she wanted and needed was someone to listen to her and accept, or validate, her feelings in the matter. I failed totally to "feel" with her. How hard that is for the male to understand.

Equally hard to understand is that a woman doesn't think in the same process as a man. Oh, I suppose that the brain cells function in the same way all right, but how it all comes together is something else. How many times has the well-meaning husband entered into a discussion with his wife over some matter and had this happen. Things are going along beautifully for the first few minutes, and then suddenly she takes a turn in the conversation, and he hasn't the vaguest idea where she went! To her, it's perfectly logical and clear, but to him, it makes no sense at all. That simply illustrates the two predominate thought patterns of male and female. A man tends to think in logical, straight-line patterns and sequence. He moves from A to B and then to C, etc. A woman is apt to jump from B all the way over to F or G, and the man doesn't even know how she got there.

There are a lot of old jokes around about woman's intuition. Actually, they only reflect an observation made by someone a long time ago about human nature. That is, that women tend to think intuitively rather than logically. As a result, the thought patterns of one sex make little sense to the other. In marriage, this often creates misunderstanding and conflict. Mary and I were hung up at this point until it occurred to us that this was a blessing in disguise.

"Honey, I just don't see this thing like that. Why can't you see it like I do? It's so simple," I would often complain.

"Maybe that's really it," Mary exclaimed. "Maybe *I can't* see it like you!" Then it hit us. It wasn't that Mary wouldn't see it my way. It was that she *couldn't*, and what a difference that is.

That difference led us to a new appreciation for what God does when He joins a man and a woman in marriage. Among a myriad of other things He accomplishes, He joins two totally different problem-solving devices—a male mentality and a female mentality. When Mary and I finally quit resenting our difference at this point, we learned to put *both* kinds of problem-solving methods to work for us! We had twice the power in working things out. There is a delicious kind of oneness and sense of unity that comes from sharing a secret like this. Learning to depend on each other's ability had led to a new level of intimacy for us.

And then, of course, intimacy is also achieved through our sexuality. The first attempts between Mary and myself to recapture sexual intimacy were both tender and ridiculously funny. Those first fumbling attempts in the motel rooms on passes from the hospital were duplicated again and again during the first months at home.

A lot of the awkwardness was deeper than just accommodating physical changes and the presence of mechanical gadgets that kept getting in the way. We had awkward *feelings* we didn't know how to handle.

When I would have recurring fears about hurting Mary by rolling over on a paralyzed arm and crushing it, or by being too aggressive and passionate, bits of conversation ensued that often left us with puzzled, hurt feelings.

"Are you okay?" I would ask, thinking I had perhaps doubled up a helpless hand under my body weight as we lay close together. My fear that I would injure her in some way was incessant. "Of course," she would reply, while thinking, *What's the matter? Isn't it good for him? Is something wrong? Maybe, I can't bring him pleasure any longer?* Her imagination would play ghastly, torturous tricks on her.

With fears like these racing through our minds, we both began to experience devastating symptoms. Mary would feel desolate in what she believed to be an inadequacy to please and excite me sexually. Her own sexual desire would fade in the face of this.

Meanwhile, I was experiencing a sense of panic. She was getting unresponsive. *Am I not enough of a man to keep her interest, to excite her, and stimulate her? What's happening to me?* An instant of that kind of questioning was all that was necessary to block all sexual response on my part. In moments like that, my whole masculinity was at stake, and I was rapidly losing the battle!

Out of such troubled moments, important lessons emerged. We eventually found—after nearly losing our sex life altogether—that communication of real feelings was *absolutely essential.* If I feared injury to her, it was necessary for me to communicate that feeling rather than to ask some veiled question that might trigger misconceptions in Mary's mind. How could she know what I really meant unless I was more explicit? We began to see how complicated a business

Communication is a complex affair!

communication can actually be. It was so easy for a message to be decoded wrong by the receiver, even when sent with the purest intent by the sender. Ever have an experience like that? Of course you have. You've blurted out some exclamation prompted by a moment of frustration or fear, only to have it totally misunderstood by the other person. Worse yet, it may even have caused resentment, though certainly no animosity was intended on your part. Bewildered, you wondered what had happened. Communication is a complex affair!

Learning the importance of communication and then being driven to learn how to communicate brought a new dimension of intimacy to our marriage. Not only did we learn to transmit true feelings about sex to each other, but we found that what we learned about communication affected other areas of our marriage as well. We could talk more freely and openly about money matters, plans for a vacation, colors for redecorating the living room, and other things. And in every one of these conversations we feel drawn together in a warm, loving sense of intimacy. Naturally, we haven't resolved all areas of conflict automatically just because we can communicate better now. Mary is still a "blue-pink-lavender" person who adds to these spring pastels a preference for "winter colors" such as red, black and white. I'm still a "fall color" person who is more comfortable with brown, orange, and yellow, and who adds more difficulty with a preference for "earth colors" in the deep greens and reddish browns. Just try to decorate a room with that combination!

Not a little of the awkwardness we felt in our sexual adjustment was because of a peculiar "hangup" of my own. In the "days of dirty diapers" when our two children were yet small, I had been a student in seminary graduate school and only able to work part time in a church. Mary had sought part-time work too, just to help keep us afloat financially. I took a share in caring for the little ones, including washing the dirty diapers each week. Before the days of disposable diapers, or of income sufficient to engage a diaper service, that meant an arduous task for me. My personal makeup rebelled at the very smell of soiled diapers! There were times when changing the baby and wiping a dirty bottom caused nausea for me. Crazy? Sure! But real, nonetheless, for whatever hidden childhood cause. (Maybe sometime a psychiatrist will find something in my potty training to account for this strange little quirk!)

Later, however, when Mary required total personal care at home, I was frequently the only one available to care for her toileting needs. The most difficult moment for me to handle was just before bedtime. There were times when I had thoughts about Mary all day long, wanting her with a normal, loving desire. In my mind, I had planned toward a beautiful experience of sex together in bed that night. I might have even unconsciously done some of the right things in preparing her emotionally through the day. But leaning over the toilet wiping a dirty bottom would wreck everything! Try as I might, I could not sustain interest in sex at such a time. My crazy hangup over smells would shut down everything that had built up throughout the day.

For a considerable time, neither Mary nor I understood what was happening. It was devastating to her for me to turn

93

suddenly cool and disinterested after a day-long "build-up" for sex. For me, it was maddening. I hated the struggle that was going on inside me. All too often that anger was directed toward Mary. I would be just a little too abrupt in helping her into bed and just a bit too rough in strapping on the shell.

But again, this eventually led to two very important insights about ourselves. The first is that sex is about 85 to 90 *percent attitudinal.* That is, it is much more controlled between the eyes than between the legs! The brain can control all sexual response and arousal. For example, one night when things were really going well and both of us were experiencing delightful arousal and response, suddenly one of the children made a noise in another part of the house.

"What was that?" Mary asked, pulling back slightly in my arms.

"I don't know," I responded, almost sitting upright in bed. The fear that one of the children might walk in on our lovemaking caused sexual desire to drain from us both almost instantly. Once the potential threat was removed by my getting up to check on the children and to lock the bedroom door, sexual arousal was once more possible—but only then! The times that such things have happened to any couple are legion.

The other thing we learned about ourselves is the importance of physical touch to sustain romantic feelings. There is a delightful little book by Dorothy T. Samuel called *Fun and Games in Marriage.*[4] The author suggests the importance of physical touch and even recommends a couple bump into each other in the hallway once in a while "accidentally." Reading this playful, yet helpful, little book gave me a new insight about our marriage and the personal hangup I had about smells. I learned that by pushing beyond the first revulsion at caring for Mary's toileting I could resolve the problem of fading sexual desire.

Touching her was the answer! After the toileting was completed, I needed simply to push through those first feelings and hold or touch or caress her. Natural sexual arousal followed. That seems so simple that anyone should have been able to see it, yet in the midst of the inner conflict I had known over this whole thing, even the obvious had become obscure.

Since rediscovering the power of physical touch, we have both deliberately sought contact with each other much more frequently in order to communicate love and tenderness. But there were still many other things Mary and I needed to learn about love and intimacy. One was the importance of focusing on the sexual needs of each other to find real fulfillment for ourselves.

The key to this concept is found in the words of Jesus to His disciples on one occasion. To be sure, He was talking about something quite different from marriage, but He laid down a life principle in the words spoken that day. The principle applies to every area of life, including marriage. He said, "'For whosoever will save his life shall lose it: and whosoever will lose his life for my sake shall find it'" (Matthew 16:25). That sounds like a riddle!

What He actually was saying was that to find happiness and fulfillment in life, one must give oneself away. One cannot find happiness in life by pursuing happiness. It will always elude you. Countless numbers of disillusioned people can attest to that. Happiness is a by-product of something else.

When you look at the great people in history who have found fulfillment in life, you discover they all have one thing in common. Though you may examine the lives of such diverse people as Alexander the Great, Madame Curie, David Livingstone, or Thomas Edison, you will find that each carries this one common element: each lost himself or herself in life to a great idea or a great cause. In losing themselves to that great idea or cause, they found fulfillment for themselves. That's the way fulfillment, or happiness, works. It sort of creeps up on you unaware. When you are least concerned about it, you discover one day in the midst of losing yourself that you are really very content.

That's the principle Jesus was emphasizing to His disciples. That life principle works just as well in marriage too. It even works in sex.

For some time, it has been known that women tend to find a degree of satisfaction sexually just in the knowledge that their mate has been fulfilled. A woman who rarely reaches orgasm discovers a quiet kind of contentment lying in the arms of her husband as she is aware that he is satisfied.

What we have only more recently come to appreciate is that men, too, reach a higher degree of satisfaction in the sex act if they have the feeling that they have brought their mate to fulfillment. Thus, if a man and woman each come to sex with the goal of the other's satisfaction in mind, they each find greater satisfaction for themselves.

Giving oneself to this principle may take many forms. It might be the gentleness with which the husband enters into love play before intercourse. It may be the expression of tenderness in loving words during the sex act. It may be just consideration for the other in not making ill-timed demands. It certainly will be in understanding that "sex begins in the kitchen and not in the bedroom," as one of my counselor friends often says. He emphasizes that the woman needs preparation time to fully enter into sex. She cannot find a high degree of satisfaction, nor give herself freely, if sex is too abrupt. The wise husband, therefore, who is thinking about something developing later that night, begins early in the day to prepare his wife for a happy sexual experience. He might call her at lunch to tell her he loves her. He might be especially attentive at dinner. He will give time to her during the evening, instead of the television set or the newspaper. All of this is simply directed toward meeting a basic need of hers to *feel loved* by her husband, and it is working out the principle of giving oneself for the other.

Mary and I are still learning about ourselves and our marriage, even after twenty-six years. Most of what we have learned took time to discover. For example, only a year ago did I stumble onto the importance of the *process* of our adjusting and readjusting to each other to the process called a marriage.

Something happened that will be very familiar to anyone who has lived in the same household with a physically handicapped person. The night of its occurrence I was so troubled by the incident that afterwards I couldn't sleep. As I thought about it I began to see it in new perspective. I got out of bed and went into the living room to write down what I was beginning to see, lest the whole thing escape me before morning. What follows is what I wrote that night:

Tonight, I felt a conflict within that arose for the many hundredth time. The conflict of feeling trapped by a situation that offers no way of escape. Yet feeling at the same time that escape from the situation is not what I want either.

We went to bed tonight at a little after eleven. I was just dozing off into sleep when Mary called out, "Keith!" I responded drowsily, "Yes, what is it?"

"Will you check my pressure on the machine?"

I got up and adjusted the pressure on the respirator, then fell back into bed hoping to drop off quickly to sleep.

Thirty minutes later, Mary called again, "Keith, I need the bed pan!"

I fought my way back to at least half wakefulness and went into the bathroom for the needed pan and tissue. When the necessity was cared for I slumped back into bed as Mary said a quiet "Thank you!" I didn't even respond.

Would you believe I was feeling really hostile that she had called me to get up these two times? In my mind, I was carrying on this dialogue with her explaining all about the impossible situation in which I was immersed.

Honey, I was saying in my head, *I just can't live with this! I have to get more rest at night. My job is demanding. Dealing with people's emotional problems all day leaves me really drained. I simply can't function if I can't get enough sleep. It's not a matter of casting blame about this or anything. It's just the same as your necessity to have the bed pan when you need it. You need to go. . . . I need to sleep!*

While this was going on, I envisioned possible solutions to the problem. I could sleep in another bedroom. But that would be ridiculous! Who would be there to care for her needs if she awoke? Well, the housekeeper would sleep in the same room with her. She would hear and respond. No, that would be stupid! What kind of a marriage would that be with me sleeping in another room? I began to feel guilty for even entertaining the idea, yet I was feeling trapped. What way could I go? The whole process of feeling sorry for myself in this situation made me feel crummy.

Well, I had some choices. I could select one of several. I could choose to do what my fantasy had devised and move to another bedroom. That would probably be a great way to write "finis" over my marriage!

I could choose to walk out on the whole thing. That would end the problem, all right! It would also end twenty-five years of marriage and destroy a couple of people in the process. Whether I liked the trapped feeling or not, I realized that neither Mary nor I could very well survive without each other. We couldn't make it without each other physically after all these years, to say nothing of our emotional need for one another.

Well, I could choose to continue as I was—enduring these occasional bouts with self-pity, guilt, and "crummi-ness." Was that all there was to choose from?

In a perceptive book, *Love and Will,* Rollo May has written a paragraph that summarizes where I find myself in the midst of this dilemma. He says, "No writer writes out of having found the answer to the problem; he writes rather out of his having the problem and wanting a solution. The solution consists not of a resolution. It consists of the deeper and wider dimension of consciousness to which the writer is carried by virtue of his wrestling with the problem...The contribution which is given to the world by the...book is the process of the search."[5]

Somewhere in the search for the answer to this quandary—one which I somehow feel is duplicated with perhaps slightly different detail in the lives of countless numbers of couples who grapple with physical handicap— there comes a "deeper and wider dimension of consciousness" just in wrestling with the problem. There comes to us all who have faced this "entrapment by circumstance" a still new way of dealing with the matter. It comes to us so that we do not just go on enduring. We may choose to turn the whole endurance contest into good. That we can somehow use this for our own betterment occurs in the recesses of our mind. Just how that is to be accomplished is not always clear, but it gives us a new attitude with which to approach the problem. Maybe we don't always need solutions to our problems, anyway. Maybe the "contribution which is given" is the process.

And what of Mary and her feelings in all of this? Did she sense the hostility I felt as I pushed back the closet door too abruptly to disclose the respirator and its pressure gauge? Could she sense something as I flipped on the flashlight and stabbed at the darkness with its slender beam? What feelings came over her as I too noisily made my way to the bathroom, secured the bed pan and tissue and came back to wait upon her necessity? The covers went back too quickly. Movement was just too abrupt. Could she sense all this?

Of course she could! You could cut the atmosphere with a knife! I wasn't hiding my feelings from her. But how would she respond to those feelings? Shame? Hurt? Anger? Frustration? Hot tears in her eyes? Maybe, some of all those things. For she, too, was sensing the feelings of being trapped.

I didn't ask to have this horrible polio! I wouldn't impose on you for your help if I could do it any other way! She might have been feeling. *I have to have the pressure adjusted; I have to have a bed pan to help myself; what else can I do? Yet I am resented by the very one I want to have love me. Is that fair? Do I deserve that?* Often, the tears had come to her eyes in the dark hours of night after I had fallen clumsily back into bed without acknowledging her "thank you." What was she to do? How could she escape the feeling of being trapped by her circumstances?

Her choices were something like mine, I suppose, and she elected to stay with the marriage, to "hang in there," for the same reasons I have chosen again and again to remain. For the same reasons that both she and I will choose again and again and again in the future to do the same. Every day brings the same array of choices. Oh, the circumstances of the day may differ, but the choices are still the same. We may not always even understand fully why we choose to remain. Maybe, we don't have to be too clear about it all. Maybe, the very lack of clarity in the situation and the choice lends validity and strength to our marriage. There's something of an act of faith involved in staying with something even if your only reason is because you just know you should. But it's in the very knowing of that that you bring incredible fiber and strength to the relationship called marriage. It has something to do with commitment.

sharing faith

"I'm never going to be able to do it! I'll never walk again! Probably *never* get out of this horrible hospital. I wish I could just *die!*" Maxine cried out the anguish of so many who had been patients at Rancho Los Amigos Hospital in Downey, California, in those early days. For many, it was a hopeless business. What point was there to exercise in physical therapy until you felt exhausted, or to learn the use of all the different equipment pieces, or to go through the months of agony to retrain muscles to do a totally different job in the body if there was no longer any-one to share your special little triumphs? What's the use if nobody cares?

For many young women there at Rancho Hospital, that was precisely the situation. Like Maxine and Millie, their husbands and families had deserted them. After the weeks had lengthened into months, well-meaning friends had grad-ually come less and less often to visit, and then not at all. It wasn't just that the future looked bleak—there didn't even seem to be a future!

Into this hopelessness, God brought my remarkable wife, Mary. Her simple, childlike faith refused to even entertain the idea that she wouldn't be well someday. She greeted each new day with eagerness and enthusiasm. From her respirator,

> *"Don't give up. God hasn't left you."*

she emanated a special kind of sunshine to all the Maxines and Millies in the ward. All eight young women in that ward had comparable involvement and paralysis from polio, but only one had a faith that God still cared.

"You *can* do it; you will leave the hospital someday, Maxine," Mary kept encouraging. "Don't give up. God hasn't left you. He still loves you and wants to give you a whole new life!" That was hard for Maxine to accept. Her husband had left her the day she entered the hospital five years before. Yet, Maxine watched her new friend Mary demonstrate convincingly that faith could make a difference. Mary, too, "had her moments," to be sure. Moments when the radiant, hopeful spirit flagged. Moments when the seriousness of her situation gripped her with dread. This wasn't an ordinary illness and hospitalization. This was turning out to be "for keeps," and she wasn't Superwoman. Sometimes, lonely and discouraged, she cried softly in the long, quiet hours of night, yet, to Maxine, she seemed somehow different from the others. There was a deep, gentle inner strength and hope. She had "something" the others didn't. There had to be something to this faith in Jesus that Mary kept alluding to. This faith—whatever it was—really did give Mary resources no one else in the ward seemed able to tap. Gradually, as the weeks went by, Maxine longed to share it.

This was a classic demonstration of the work of the Holy Spirit through a single, committed life. Totally encased in the respirator most of the time, Mary had no access to a

Bible with which she could strengthen her witness. She had to simply rely on the many verses and passages committed to memory as a small girl in Sunday school. The Holy Spirit brought them all back. Verse after verse from the Psalms of David spilled forth hope and encouragement. Again and again, the words of Jesus from the Gospels brought the tenderness of a loving heavenly Father into that hospital room. Forgiveness moved with gentleness into troubled, anxious hearts.

"Let Jesus take away all the bitterness and hurt you're feeling," Mary counseled. "Maxine, ask Him to do it! He will! You don't *need* to have that heavy thing to carry around inside of you. You and I have enough other problems to face without that too!"

The inner healing that God brought to those women through Mary was without doubt a major factor in their progress toward feelings of wholeness and worth, of hope for a future with meaning.

Even the nurses and therapists received the touch of God's love through Mary. Liz, a lovely, red-headed therapist, was like so many others who, when near Mary, unconsciously demonstrated a wistful longing for "the something more" that Mary seemed to possess.

"How do you keep your buoyant spirit, Mary?" Liz questioned. "I never see you 'down' like the others! I wish I could know your secret."

"It's no secret, Liz," Mary replied. "My Father in Heaven reminds me every day of how much He loves me, and that just keeps me *singing* on the inside. He loves me

"My Father in Heaven reminds me every day of how much He loves me..."

and will take care of me. I know everything is going to be all right. I wish you could know Him and His love too!"

The remarkable part of all this was that Mary was totally unaware of the profound influence she was exerting. But then, most real saints, I suppose, are not especially conscious of their saintliness. After all, calling attention to one's halo rather spoils the whole thing!

The lives that God enriched there in the hospital through this unpretentious young woman were only the first of an ever-lengthening file of persons. At home, after those grueling thirteen months of hospitalization, the need for housekeepers to "live in" provided a steady stream of persons whose lives were also affected. As woman after woman came to live in our home to care for Mary and our family, each encountered someone different from anyone they had known before.

It was tedious, at best, for both the housekeepers and Mary. Many of the housekeeping aides were mature, older women who had already managed their own homes for a number of years. It was difficult for them to adjust to doing things the way someone else would do them. On the other hand, there was nothing wrong with Mary's mind and capacity to feel, reason, and plan. She knew how she wanted her household run. She just couldn't do it without someone else's hands. Eventually, I even began to tell the housekeepers that they were with us primarily to be Mary's hands. "I want her to feel that she is completely in charge of her home," I said to them. "It's important that she feels that sense of capability. And if she tells you to do something in a way that's different from the way you're accustomed to doing it, never mind. Just do it her way. If it succeeds, well and good. If it doesn't, then it's not your problem! If the cake turns out terrible, for instance, it's not your fault. I want her to have a sense of full responsibility."

But can you imagine what it's like to have someone else brush your teeth? Or tell someone else how to make a soufflé? Or enchiladas?

And how do you instruct someone about pulling on your girdle? How do you manage the right tug here, and straighten the wrinkle there, through someone else's hands? Have you ever had another person give you a drink of water from a glass? Initially, they tip it too much, or not enough, or to one side, or the other. There are several ways they can pour the water all over your chin and onto the fresh new blouse the two of you have just struggled to put on! Donning a wig can be hilariously funny or hopelessly frustrating when you're using someone else's hands to do it. It has been said that no one can ever put someone else's hat on satisfactorily. Just try a wig!

It's truly amazing how many ways there are to put pots and pans away in a cupboard, and how many variations there can be to setting a dinner table. In spite of the frustration of adjusting to such things, however, Mary found it possible to share her faith with these women. It was as though God had arranged to bring a series of persons into her life who needed to know Him, and He was working through Mary to reveal Himself to them. Our bathroom became a sort of counseling center. Many long, life-changing conversations have taken place while the housekeeper bathed and dressed Mary for the day.

One lovely young girl was a good example. Bridgett had only been in America less than six months when she came to work for us. Much of our American way of life was still new to her. Even more new to her was the knowledge of God's love for her, demonstrated in Jesus Christ. It was through Mary's simple, childlike belief that she too came to personal faith in Christ. Mary shared again and again how Jesus had helped her cope with handicap and helplessness. Bridgett is now married and has a home and family of her own, but the new life she began as Mary introduced her to Jesus has continued as a transforming power in her life and that of her family. How thrilling that a totally handicapped lady could so rise above her own limitations to minister to another. Then, the results of that investment of self and of love could move outward to still others, like the ripples in a pond, in a never ending, ever increasing circle of influence. Certainly, no one ever has to feel that he or she is shut off from life, from significance, by a physical handicap that makes one a prisoner in one's own home. Through even one other person who enters that home, the handicapped has an open door of influence upon the world.

One day, Vivian, a little neighbor girl, came to Mary and said, "My mother wants to know if you'll help me learn to read better."

"Well I don't know if I can," Mary replied. "Let me talk to your mommy, and then we'll see."

That little conversation began an entirely new episode in our lives.

Mary accepted Vivian as a student and began to work with her after school and on Saturdays. I went to the public library and secured some books on remedial reading techniques. One of these, *The Writing Road to Reading*, by Romalda and Walter Spalding, turned out to be a jewel.[6] It described a highly workable program that Mary utilized with incredible success.

Soon, little Vivian began to show marked improvement in reading skill. Before long, she was in the top reading group in her class at the school across the street from our house. Her mother was ecstatic. She told all her friends about the wonderful tutor who was helping Vivian. Soon, other mothers were calling Mary to arrange tutoring for their children.

Before long, I found the house a beehive of activity in late afternoon and Saturdays. Children and mothers were coming and going at intervals all day long.

Word began to filter from parents who were delighted at the progress of their children to teachers who began to question parents about the obvious changes in both ability and attitudes of their children. From the teachers, word came to the principal about the remarkable lady in the wheelchair who lived across the street from the school and who was tutoring children in remedial reading. Then, the principal telephoned Mary.

"Mrs. Korstjens, I've been hearing about the unusual success you've been having in tutoring some of our children.

The parents and teachers are simply delighted. I'd like to meet you and talk with you about your work. Is there any way you could possibly come across the street to my office sometime?"

"Why, yes, I suppose so," Mary replied. "I think my housekeeper could bring me across the street." So an appointment was arranged.

The principal was so gratified by the solid, fundamental approach to phonics that Mary employed that she asked her to come to the school a couple of days each week to take youngsters right from the classroom for tutoring. A separate room was provided, and children who had special problems were sent to Mary during their regular reading periods.

While not every student responded with a dramatic increase in ability, those who were not handicapped by a neurological disorder did make significant progress—enough so that the principal shared the whole story of her school at the Central Office of Pomona City Schools.

Then, our telephone went berserk! Parents from all over the city began calling to engage this wonderworker. There was just no way that Mary could accept all the requests that were made.

Out of all this excitement and fervor, something else was growing, too. Each child who came to our house brought a mother! Gradually, Mary began to relate to the mothers. At first, it was just to have them remain a moment after the tutoring session to discuss their children's progress and home assignments. Little by little, however, she noted that the mothers stayed longer to talk to her about other things.

"Mary, I shouldn't tell you about this," one young mother confided, "but somehow I've got to talk to somebody about it. Can I ask you about a . . . about a personal problem?"

"Of course," Mary responded, quietly wondering what kind of personal problem it could be. "Well, my marriage isn't going too well," the young woman continued. "My husband and I seem to be arguing and fighting a lot lately."

And so it began. It happened like that over and over again. Mary was soon spending as much time in counseling with wives and mothers as in tutoring the children they brought.

As I watched this process, it finally dawned upon me that God had a significant task for Mary to perform. He had even arranged this second way to *bring people to her* so that the task could be carried out. In the first place, He brought women in the role of housekeepers to Mary for her help and counsel. In the second, He brought them to her as mothers of educationally handicapped children.

Mary's success in guiding and counseling these women suggested in my thinking that she could and should be sharing with even greater numbers of troubled women. But how? God had been bringing all these. Could He arrange for even more?

I believe He gave the idea. "Mary should be teaching classes for young wives and mothers," I thought. "She has so much practical knowledge and insight to share. She knows God's plan for marriage and the home so well as it is described in the Bible. She needs an opportunity to teach all of this to other women."

Getting her to feel that way about it was something else though. It was fully three years before I could convince her that she should try it. She felt she didn't have much worth sharing. "And besides," she would remonstrate, "who would want to have a teacher in a wheelchair?"

"Hey, wait a minute!" I countered. "All those gals who have been coming to you for help haven't been bothered one bit by the chair! Forget that!"

While Mary was struggling in her own mind over the possibilities of teaching, I was casting about for a basic course or textbook she might use as sort of a foundation for a course of study for young wives. When eventually I found something that I thought could be adapted, I asked Mary to read it. Even though she saw the possibilities in the text and envisioned innumerable ways she could strengthen its message from her own knowledge and experience, she was still unwilling to assume the role of a teacher. It just seemed to her rather presumptuous to believe that she could be of help to anyone, yet scores of women had already been seeking her loving counsel during those preceding months.

Finally, she hesitatingly agreed. "Okay," she said, "but I really don't know what I'm getting into!" We prayed a lot after that, asking the Lord to guide Mary in preparation for this new venture.

We set up the first classes under the auspices of the Family Life Department of the church in Pomona where I serve. Twelve women enrolled for the day class, and ten signed up for the night class.

Mary couldn't believe what happened. In sharing in the group each week, the women began to recount how their own attitudes toward their husbands were changing and how their marriages were getting better and better. One "graduate" of her first class wrote in her evaluation of the experience, "This course has saved my marriage! My husband and I had already agreed a week before classes began that we were going to get a divorce. Now, we've found each other all over again, and we're going to work out our problems together. Thank God for you, Mary!"

We cried tears of gratitude together when we read that note, and that note became a little confirmation from God that what Mary was doing was the right thing after all.

The graduates of her classes have grown in number from those first twenty-two to hundreds of women throughout our Southern California region in the intervening few years. What a lesson we both learned of what God can do when we're willing to let Him. And God also takes seemingly little, unimportant things and uses them in such striking ways. He uses even letters that we write, for instance.

Learning to write again while still in the hospital had been a struggle. Mary's first attempts to write even simple notes had been tedious and painstaking. A letter written to anyone then meant two or three hours of carefully formed characters filling only a single page. To even grasp the pen, Mary needed help to make the necessary pinch between thumb and first finger. A short arm brace provided this needed assistance. The movement for writing and forming characters into words was more complicated. The arm muscles no longer functioned, so others that were still operational had to be trained to do this unfamiliar task. Muscles of the body trunk had to be carefully retrained to operate an arm tray. This ingenious gadget is a multi-hinged con-trivance that supported her free arm and provided move-ment both upward and downward, forward and back.

Those who received her brief letters could not help but remember the hours of tortured practice they had endured in the first grade of school, learning to properly form their letters. How awkward the pen and how strenuous the effort, yet they had full use of their fingers, hand, and arm. How family and close friends treasured those first letters Mary wrote! Gradually, writing became easier for her and letters more numerous. Another kind of personal ministry was beginning to take shape. It was a ministry of letter writing.

Perhaps, it was partly inspired by Hazel Fox. Hazel is a delightful little lady in our congregation who determined several years ago that she would take for herself a ministry of *encouragement*. She writes little notes to Dr. Edward Cole, our pastor, and to other staff ministers of the church, offer-ing gentle words of encouragement at most unusual times. Almost always a note comes from Hazel Fox just at the time when one of our ministers is particularly "down" in spirit. She writes to friends and acquaintances with similar little uplifting messages. The timing of the Holy Spirit in prompt-ing her to write is uncanny.

One such note came to me in the midst of a particularly trying time. I shared the note with Mary at home that night. "Honey, you have to read this. It's a note from Hazel Fox, the little lady who lives in the apartments over on Gordon Street. How she could have known that I needed just these words, I don't know unless the Lord told her! Anyway, it's something very special."

Mary read the lovely note and then sat, quiet and pensive, for a long while. Finally, she said rather hesitantly, "You know, Keith, this note has really convicted me. I'm sure that Hazel didn't intend any such thing to happen, but I just realized that I have time...more time perhaps than most people. And what am I doing with it? I could be writing notes of encouragement to folks, too."

Actually, Mary had been doing more with letter writing than she was aware already. The first notes and letters had been to family members and close friends, of course. Early in their childhood, Kenneth and Karen grew accustomed to receiving special letters from Mother on birthdays and other significant occasions. Neither Mary nor I knew whether these letters were meaningful to our children or not until years later when we discovered that they had carefully preserved *every letter*! Those letters seemed to be a curiously effective way of reaching the children. When Kenneth was grown to high-school-football size of six feet tall and 210 pounds, he still treasured notes from Mom. They invariably clouded his eyes with tears.

Later, close friends were touched by the richness and simplicity of these notes, too. When our dear friend Joyce Landorf experienced the death of her mother, Mary wrote to Joyce out of love and understanding. The note wasn't long or particularly profound. It was just a simple expression of tender love and concern, but it carried special meaning to Joyce, who later included it in her book *Mourning Song*.[7] In that book, she wrote so poignantly of her own experience of dealing with the death of her mother and little baby boy.

Mary had written:

Dearest Joyce,

You and your family are on my mind and heart so much these days.

   The book of poems by Martha Snell Nicholson that you lent me once had two poems I have enclosed. They were very precious to me when my mom went to be with God. Joyce, may God's love sustain and strengthen you beyond belief.

All my love and prayers,
Mary

One of the two poems she had carefully copied into the letter was this:

THE HEART HELD HIGH

God made me a gift of laughter
And a heart held high,
Knowing what life would bring me
By and by,

Seeing my roses wither
One by one,
Hearing my life-song falter,
Scarce begun,

Watching me walk with Sorrow. . . .
That is why
He made me this gift of laughter
This heart held high.[8]

Joyce knew something of the pain and suffering of the lady who had originally penned these words. She couldn't help but see, too, how the words "Hearing my life-song falter/Scarce begun" echoed the heart-cry of one whom she knew even more personally. She knew that Mary understood the devastation of crumbled, broken life plans and dreams and the crushing impact of irretrievable loss. Written from that vantage point of

...the strength and simplicity of this remarkable lady's faith keeps shining.

personal experience, Mary's simple little note to Joyce carried great encouragement and strength.

Scores of people have known the touch of this radiant life in a similar way. Through it all—whether sharing faith and counsel with numerous housekeepers over the years or counseling troubled mothers of educationally handicapped children or teaching hundreds of young wives to more happily fulfill their roles as wife and mother or writing to people across the country—the strength and simplicity of this remarkable lady's faith keeps shining.

What's it like to be married to such a woman? Let me tell you—it's a delight! There's nothing stodgy or super-pious about her. Her faith is demonstrated so unassumingly that you are immersed in its healing effects almost without awareness. It's a little like an incident that happened at church one day.

Mary couldn't quite manage all the demands of being a teacher of small children in Sunday school class, but she did accept the responsibility of becoming a secretary of the kindergarten four-year-olds. Eleanor (Happi) Moore, the department director, had convinced her that the task of record-keeping could be streamlined enough for Mary to handle the job efficiently.

The unexpected benefit that came with this arrangement was the rapidity with which Mary related to the children. It seemed uncanny. The gentleness in her manner and the softness and simplicity in her speech drew the children. Every child was individually recognized and received.

"Hello, Donald," she would greet the earliest comer on Sunday morning. "I'm so glad you're here again today bright and early. You'll have time even before the story time to listen to the records you like so much. Aren't we glad that our Heavenly Father loves us enough to give us a happy Sunday school like this? You can go right in now, Donald, and Miss Pinky will help you find the records you like best."

"Good morning, Shelley," she would greet the next arrival. "I think you must have brought something to share this morning, didn't you? Tell me about what you brought."

"It's my new pet turtle. His name is Hector. Daddy brought him home from his trip," Shelley would respond.

"My, Hector is shy, isn't he? He keeps his head tucked back under his shell a lot," Mary might observe. "The boys and girls will be happy to meet Hector this morning. Miss Peggy will probably help you find a place where Hector will be comfortable and happy this morning."

The children gravitated to her like metal filings to a magnet!

Perhaps, a part of the phenomenon was the curiosity that Mary's wheelchair aroused in little minds, but certainly a far greater part was just the fact that she was physically positioned at the children's level. They could look right into her face and eyes when they talked to her. She was down in their world.

Gradually, the novelty of the wheelchair disappeared from the minds of each child as each came to accept Miss Mary, as she was known to them, matter-of-factly. She was simply the smiling, lovely lady who greeted each one by his or her first name each Sunday morning.

One day, the teacher talked with the boys and girls about people in their lives who are "helpers." The class discussed many kinds of people who help us daily, such as policemen and firemen and the crossing guard at the school crosswalk. Then, the teacher asked each one to draw a picture of someone who was a "helper."

As they shared their pictures later, one little girl showed the picture she had drawn of a lady standing by the door.

"Tell us about your helper, Susan," the teacher encouraged.

"This is Miss Mary," Susan replied. "She helps us every Sunday. She makes us feel glad to come to Sunday school!"

"That's right, Susan, Miss Mary is a helper. I notice that Miss Mary is standing up in your picture, Susan. Where is her wheelchair?"

"Oh," Susan exclaimed, wide-eyed as her hand flew to her mouth, *"I forgot all about the wheelchair!"*

Susan was just like everyone else who is around Mary. One quickly forgets that she is in a wheelchair. There is such a positive, wholesome and healing character to her life and faith that everyone surrounding her is unaware of the chair and immersed in a life!

finding goals

"Keith, do you realize how much we've changed over the past few years?" Mary asked me one day. "Neither of us is the same person we were when we married. We're not even the same as when I came home from the hospital a few years ago. If we're changing this much, I wonder where we are headed."

"I guess I haven't given too much thought to that," I confessed. "What do you mean?"

"Well, do we *know* where we're going with this marriage? Do we have any goals? Any direction?"

"You know," I said, "I don't suppose it had ever occurred to me that a marriage should have any goals. I guess I've been like most other people who just thought of *getting married* as the goal! Maybe, we really do need to think about this. Practically all other areas of our life are goal-oriented, and successes have pretty much been achieved by setting and reaching those goals."

The conversation launched a powerful new era in our marriage. From that, we've come to some deep convictions about goals in marriage. If there's a goal that everybody seeks to achieve, I suppose it's the goal of happiness. That could be truly called a universal goal. But what is it? It means such different things to different people.

121

I saw a bumper sticker the other day that said, "Happiness is a warm puppy." There's another one around these days that says, "Happiness is being single." It seems that happiness depends a lot on one's point of view, yet everybody wants it. How do you get it?

Earlier, when we were talking about love and intimacy, we suggested that real fulfillment in life could only be found in giving oneself away. It was noted that the great personalities of history have frequently demonstrated the truth of Jesus' words, "Whosoever will save his life shall lose it: and whosoever will lose his life...shall find it" (Matthew 16:25). Happiness is a by-product of this self-giving way of life.

If there is any single word that is a near equivalent to the biblical concept of loving, it is the word *giving*. It is this selfless giving that brings true happiness. Reaching for happiness in marriage will be futile without first learning from the Nazarene Carpenter the nature of true, selfless love.

One day, I asked a young engaged couple who had come to see me why they wanted to get married. They responded, "We're in love!" That has such a beautiful sound—especially to me, a hopeless romantic! But I had to ask them, "What is love? Tell me about it."

Usually, when I ask that question, the answers have something to do with good feelings each is experiencing toward the other. Some will add the desire to be near the other. A few will even suggest love has something to do with pleasing the other person. Few, however, can give anything like a comprehensive definition of love.

I'm not really surprised. The poets have been trying to do that for centuries, and even they haven't been able to do justice to the subject matter. Probably the only way one can give definition to love at all is to examine its components or parts. When one gains a more complete view of all the parts that make up mature love, then the whole becomes more clearly defined.

I gave this young couple, Ben and Susie, a sheet of paper with a crudely drawn circle on the front. I then divided the circle into segments like the following:

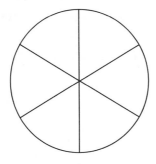

Then I said to them, "Each of you alternately write the name of one of the components or parts of love as you understand it in each of the pie-shaped segments." As soon as they caught on to the idea, the contributions came quickly. They recorded such things as respect, trust, companionship, sharing, caring, and responsibility. It occurred to them that the list could get quite long, given a little time to develop it. Mature love is a complex thing.

Somewhere along the line, Ben wrote in "sex." And, of course, he was quite right. That is a part of it. Physical attraction accounts for perhaps ten to fifteen percent of the experience we call "love."

> ...we do not "fall" in love— we "grow" in love!

"Now that we've filled up the segments in the circle," I said to the couple, "I want you to find any parts that happen to us instantaneously."

As they examined the circle, they found only one element that happens instantly. That is physical attraction.

"That's the kind of thing," I said, "that happens to some as they walk into a crowded room and are instantly attracted to one person of the opposite sex in all that crowd of people. It is the natural affinity that maleness has for femaleness and vice versa. It's a powerful thing, a beautiful thing, and I'm glad God thought it up! It's the only thing that happens 'on the spur of the moment.'

"All the others," I continued, "suggest a sequence of events. For example, it takes a sequence of events—of things that happen between two people—for one to prove the quality of trustworthiness and, thereby, elicit trust from the other. The same is true of respect. Companionship just naturally implies a series of events or times in which two people are together. So, too, does sharing."

As we talked about that, they began to gain a new insight into love: we do not "fall" in love—we "grow" in love!

"That's quite an upsetting idea to a young couple who has always held a very vague, sentimental view of love," I continued, "and there's even a more upsetting corollary to that maxim. That is, the sequence of events required for these elements to materialize and grow also requires a series of decisions on the part of the persons involved. At each event in the series, each person must decide if he or she will act in a positive, loving manner toward the other person or in a negative, unloving manner. In a sense, by these decisions we deliberately create the climate in which love can grow. We do it by our choices!"

"How does that really work?" asked Ben.

"Well, for example," I replied, "there are any number of beautiful women who come to me for counseling. As they sit in my office, I often feel physically attracted to them. After all, I don't have ice water in my veins! That doesn't make me some kind of a dirty old man. It simply says that I am quite normal. But what I do with that attraction is very important! I have to decide, and I'd better decide quickly before my imagination goes to work!

"You see," I continued, "there is a sequence of things taking place inside of me constantly. There is no action on my part—not even the movement of my fingers—that can take place without a thought in the brain preceding it. That thought, or command, triggers the muscles into action."

"But what does that have to do with your feelings about the beautiful blond sitting in your office?" Suzie asked.

"Well, if I *decide* to let my imagination take over at this moment, I could be in real trouble. Suppose I think to myself, 'Here is a lovely young woman who has been terribly wronged. She needs someone to listen appreciatively as she completely ventilates all the anger and hurt of this terrible situation. She needs companionship, too. We could go to

> "...love is constantly dying and must be constantly renewed."

lunch together and I could hear her out.' If I began thinking like that, what would happen?" I asked.

"You'd probably convince yourself to take her to lunch," Ben answered.

"That's exactly right," I replied. "Because every action has first been a thought entertained in the mind. So right at this point, I must make a decision. Will I think—and thus act—in a loving way to this exciting young creature, or will I act in a loving way to my wife who is waiting trustingly for me to come home to lunch? Thankfully, I'm smart enough to know how to decide!"

"Is that the way love begins to erode between two people?" Suzie asked. "As simple as that?"

"It's not simple," I suggested, "but it does begin with just such little things. You see, love is constantly dying and must be constantly renewed. Our choices in just such things as this daily bring it new life...or destroy it. That's what I meant when I said that we deliberately create the climate in which love begins and continues to grow."

"So that's what you meant by saying we don't really fall in love at all, but actually grow into love by our own choices," Ben observed.

"And we can literally set ourselves a goal of creating and growing mature love between ourselves," I continued. "That might not seem too romantic, but it is realistic and terribly important to a healthy marriage. In fact, it could well be the first and most important goal of your marriage."

Developing, nurturing, cultivating that mature love has become the most significant goal for Mary and me in our twenty-six years together. Only one thing is more important, and that is the centrality of Jesus Christ to that love. We loved each other when we were first married. In fact, we were a little "batty" about each other! But even that love couldn't measure up to the quality of the love we now share. Mature love is a worthy, perhaps universal, goal for marriage. Its growth and development, of course, must be understood. It is surprising how seldom young couples comprehend the nature of this mature love or how to make it grow.

Frequently, a young couple whose marriage is in trouble will make an appointment to talk with me. One such couple (I'll call them Fred and Linda) sat in my office while we talked about this matter of developing mature love.

Linda finally asked, "How do you do it? You've been saying to us that we should *choose* to do those things that build love, but we don't even know what those things are! We seem to do all the wrong things."

"The whole thing is a little like that big plant behind you," I answered, indicating a giant dieffenbachia behind her chair. "As long as my secretary does all the right things for that plant, it grows like a weed. If she doesn't, it immediately begins to wilt and die. Love is like that. The secret is in knowing what things will make it flourish.

"Every week my secretary gives that seven-foot-man-eater just the right amount of water, just the right amount of natural light, and lots of artificial light from these fluorescent lamps. It's grown to be over seven feet tall because its basic needs are regularly being met."

"And there are 'basic needs' of love, too?" asked Fred.

"Let's just say there are basic needs of maleness and femaleness, and when these are met, mature love can flourish in the climate that is created," I responded.

"What are those needs?" Fred persisted.

I took a piece of paper and a pencil and pulled my chair up close to theirs. "Perhaps, we can understand this more clearly from a little diagram. This idea isn't new or original with me. I got it from a counselor in Escanaba, Michigan, a man by the name of Urb Steinmetz. It really has helped hundreds of couples understand this."

On the top of the paper, I wrote "Male" on the left side and "Female" on the right. At the bottom of the page, I wrote "physical attraction" under each heading.

"All people, male and female, begin a relationship the same way," I continued. "They both begin with physical attraction. But that's where the similarity ends. They do not handle life the same from that point on. The male begins with physical attraction and moves almost immediately to sex." I drew a short arrow up from the words "physical attraction" and above it wrote "sex."

"The male is a sexual being. God wired him up that way. The ordinary male will watch every cute little bottom that walks across in front of his car at the intersection, not because he has a dirty mind or is mentally undressing her, but because he's just a typical male!"

"Is that why Fred looks at every pretty girl on the street?" Linda asked. "I thought maybe he just wasn't interested in me anymore."

"The day he quits looking," I responded, "he's dead!"

Fred grinned sheepishly.

"It has nothing to do with whether or not he's interested in you," I continued, "but everything to do with his sexual orientation to life. Naturally, we're talking in generalities here with this diagram, so not everything will fit perfectly into every situation, but most things will sound surprisingly familiar!

"Now, let's go on. If the male has a fairly satisfactory and fulfilling experience sexually, he will move to mature love. He almost always comes to mature love this way." (Another arrow drawn pointing upward with the word "love" at the top.)

"I've read somewhere that most young men marry for sex," Linda remarked. "Is that right?"

"Well, thoughtful young men today are looking for some other things in addition," I observed, "but all are looking for a bed partner. They have an extremely strong sex drive that has been held in check most of their teenage years. They are looking for sexual expression. There's nothing wrong with that. It's quite normal, remember!"

"I can accept this okay," said Fred, "but how is this different from the woman? Doesn't she want sex too? Today's woman is certainly much more free to express her sexual drive and even to be sexually aggressive."

129

"It's true that today's culture has given the woman more freedom to express her sex drive without inhibition," I returned, "and this is essentially a good thing. But she tends to handle life in a somewhat different pattern than the male. She begins in the same place with physical attraction, but she moves almost immediately to love."

I drew an arrow up from the words "physical attraction" and wrote "love" above the arrow's point.

"To her," I continued, "this means a thousand different things that make her feel secure in *being* loved—things like being held and being told that she is lovely...like silly, sentimental, little gifts that don't mean a thing to anyone in the world except her like remembering special days such as birthdays and anniversaries. And it's being told that she is loved. Every good husband needs 365 ways to say 'I love you'—one for every day of the year. The woman needs that constant reassurance of her husband's love."

"But she *knows* I love her!" Fred interrupted. "I work hard to supply all the things I know she wants. And yet she's never satisfied!"

"I don't want *things*, Fred!" Linda cried. "I want you!"

"I guess I just don't understand women," Fred admitted.

"What she's trying to say to you, Fred, is that you can't buy her enough junk to make up for her feeling really loved and being number one in your life. It takes an investment of yourself and your time to make her feel that way." I drew a final arrow pointing up from the word "love" and wrote in "sex."

"Now when a woman really feels loved—and secure in that love—she moves quite easily to a satisfactory sexual experience. She almost always comes this way too. It's very difficult for her to find fulfillment sexually without the experience of love beforehand."

"I think the diagram is really very true—for me, anyway," Linda interjected.

"It is true of most women, Linda," I said. "In order for us to meet the basic needs of each other in marriage, it's essential to understand the ideas incorporated in this diagram."

"But how do we understand about *basic needs* from this?" asked Fred.

"Well, let's go on with this for a minute," I responded.

Then, I drew a circle around the words "sex" in the Male column and "love" in the Female column. "These two words represent basic needs of maleness and femaleness," I continued. "The woman's basic need is to feel *secure* in being loved. When she has that, she has everything. Without that she has nothing, and you can't buy her enough stuff to make up for it! Many women who don't have this secure feeling begin to use sex to try to get it. After all, the only time their husbands ever tell them they love them is in the midst of intercourse. So unconsciously, they use the only tool they have to get a love response. It's kind of sick—but it happens frequently."

"What causes this weakness of being so insecure at this point?" Fred inquired.

"It's not a weakness, Fred, only a difference," I responded. "You'll see a corresponding difference in the male in a moment. Over here you see the circle around the word "sex." This has to do with the basic need of maleness."

Linda interrupted, "Well, is that all men want, sex?"

"No, Linda," I answered, "it's more complicated than that. It is related to their sex drive, but it's bigger than that. It's the need for the male to maintain satisfactory ego strength to function adequately. The most fragile thing in the universe may be the male ego! We men have a terrible time with it, though we don't readily admit it. Either the thing is entirely out of control and we are acting like egomaniacs, or it's so deflated we could crawl out under the door. Our problem is to maintain some reasonable balance."

"I don't understand what that has to do with sex," Linda said.

"Well, the male gets a part of his ego strength from his sexual performance. He has to 'perform' in the sex act. If he performs well, his ego is enhanced. If he performs poorly, he suffers humiliation, at least inwardly. His sexual performance is tied directly to his level of ego strength."

"But that's not the only source of a man's ego strength, is it?" Fred asked. "Doesn't he also derive ego building from his work, his friends and acquaintances, and even such things as community projects?"

"That's exactly right, Fred." I responded. "The important matter here is the complex need for a balanced level of ego strength. This is the basic need of male personality. Of course, it's not a weakness any more than the female need for security in being loved is. It's just a difference.

"Now, when the male has this satisfactory level of ego strength, he functions quite well. In fact, if he has this, he has everything. If he doesn't have it, he has nothing. The typical male who has an appropriate level of ego strength, or sense of masculinity, could lose all of his physical possessions today, sleep on a park bench tonight, and get up tomorrow morning ready to begin all over again. He can do this because he feels good about himself."

"What happens to him if he doesn't have this?" Linda queried.

"You've heard lots of jokes about 'henpecked husbands,' haven't you?" I asked. "They are just men who have, for one reason or another, been robbed of their sense of masculinity and wholeness. They have insufficient ego strength to fulfill their masculine role."

"Do you mean that the masculine role is the macho thing we see on TV?" Linda bristled.

"Not at all," I returned, "but it is a significantly different role from that of the female! The important thing for us here, however, is to see how we can focus in on these primary needs of maleness and femaleness as marriage partners. If we can meet these needs to any significant degree, we can provide a high level of fulfillment for our mate."

I opened a Bible which was lying on the desk to Ephesians chapter five. "The Apostle Paul may not have had all the psychological terms we have at our disposal, but he did understand about human personality. Here in his letter to the Ephesian church, he talks about the very thing we have been discussing.

"In his comments about the marriage relationship, Paul begins with the use of a phrase that scares women to death these days. They're alarmed because they don't understand the meaning of his terms. He says, 'Wives, submit yourselves unto your own husbands.' Most women envision that as becoming some sort of a doormat, and they are not about to accept that kind of a role in life! What Paul really means by submission, however, is a far different thing. Just one sentence earlier Paul has put it all in proper perspective when he has counseled the married couple to be 'submitting...one to another in the fear of God.' That doesn't sound at all like some chauvinistic attempt to reduce women to second-class citizens. The *Living Bible's* paraphrase of 1 Peter 3:1 captures Paul's meaning of submission beautifully. It reads, 'Wives, fit in with your husbands' plans.' That doesn't suggest becoming a doormat but rather becoming an *active complement* to his life. Actually, it's the same thing we've been saying. 'Fit into your husband's plans and life in such a way as to make him feel complete, whole, complemented. Offer the continuous affirmation of him as a person that he needs to maintain his ego strength, or sense of masculinity. Meet his basic need!'

"Then the Apostle turns right around and says, 'Husbands, love your wives, even as Christ also loved the church, and gave himself for it' (Ephesians 5:25). That means totally, self-sacrificially. Christ literally gave his life for the church."

"Wow!" Linda exploded. "If a woman could be loved like that by her man, she wouldn't have any trouble fitting into his life!"

"You've caught the impact of this precisely, Linda," I said. "A woman who felt *that loved* by her husband would also feel completely comfortable in making every effort to meet his needs, too! What the Apostle Paul has given us here in Ephesians is simply the direct application of all the implications of this diagram we have drawn here. Deliberately deciding to do what we can to meet the basic needs of each other in marriage is a big part of developing mature love!"

The second goal that became important to Mary and to me came out of an experience already related. It was during the period when Mary was growing so rapidly as a person in her tutoring, teaching, and counseling roles.

I had always shared with most other young ministers an awesome sense of the seriousness of a "call to the ministry." That "call" had been a very real experience for me, and I continued, over the years, to feel strangely humbled that God would pick me, of all persons, for the ministry! What I failed to realize, though, was that God wasn't calling my wife and my children also to my ministry. Any calling He would do to them would be to their own life service.

Gradually, as Mary increased in effectiveness as a tutor and then as counselor, I began to see that God had a ministry *especially for her.* It was different from mine, though it reinforced and complemented mine beautifully. It dawned on me that I *could cooperate with God* in encouraging Mary in this calling. It was then that I began to urge her earnestly to start teaching the classes. What an exciting venture to be a part of the "becoming of the other," as I eventually came

"Marriage is the process God uses to help two people become the persons He always intended them to be."

to call this experience. As we more fully understood God's plan for each of our lives, Mary and I were aware that this was an intent of God for *every* marriage. Two people could work together with God in the "becoming of the other."

I have a counselor friend, H. Norman Wright, who has given a thought-provoking definition of marriage. He says, "Marriage is the process God uses to help two people become the persons He always intended them to be." That process can be a doubly exciting matter if one senses that he or she is in partnership with Almighty God in working out His plans and purposes in the life of a mate.

Rick and Teresa were another young couple that I was privileged to counsel and to marry. They are the son and daughter-in-law of Dick and Joyce Landorf. During our sessions together, we talked about goals, and Rick said, "We want to set goals for our marriage and family life, too, but I'm not sure we know how."

"Well," I said, "what kind of children do you want to have?"

"We want healthy, happy, well-adjusted children," Teresa answered, "who know Jesus as Savior and love Him like we do."

"General Electric has a motto, I'm told," I said, "that asks the question, 'What kind of a product do you want to turn out?' That question suggests that keeping an eye on the end product helps determine how you are going to get there."

"You mean, that if we want well-behaved children," Rick interjected, "we have to pay attention to their training along the way."

"Exactly!" I said. "You have practically set forth the next universal goal that Mary and I have adopted for ourselves. That is, a climate of discipline for our home."

"What do you mean, a *climate* of discipline?" Teresa asked. "I thought climate had to do with the weather."

"It's sort of the pervading or continuing character of life in the home, I guess," I answered. "But it involves more than just the children. It involves the parents as well. They, too, must live disciplined lives as a model for their children to follow.

"By the way," I continued, "I personally believe that children develop that desirable trait of self-control only by internalizing the *external controls* of a consistent climate of discipline that surrounds them. If we fail to supply it, we condemn them to a life of social maladjustment. You have to live by some kind of rules all of your life. The climate of discipline is only one of the 'climates' to be sought. The goal of a wholesome emotional climate is worth working for. So, too, is a consistent spiritual climate. All these might be considered universal goals."

"Aren't some goals for marriage very...individual?" asked Teresa. "Not everybody thinks that even having children is desirable."

"That's true, Teresa, for some couples having a family is not one of their goals," I answered. "There is an entire body of goals that might be termed individual goals. Raising children is one of these. Financial security is another. Educational goals come under this heading. And so does buying a home. Some people would rather live in an apartment."

"But all of these are legitimate goals, aren't they?" asked Rick. "People are just different in what they want in life."

"Yes, of course," I responded. "The important part of it all is that the couple know what it is that they personally want in life and set some realistic goals that encompass those things."

"There's a richness that comes to relationships when there is sharing to reach the goal." I haven't the vaguest idea who said that, but it's certainly worth remembering! Somehow, Mary and I found increasing richness in our own marriage as we struggled together to reach our goals. I suppose it has something to do with the concept of intimacy as discussed earlier.

When you become aware, for instance, that your handicapped mate is working with deliberation to find effective substitutes for caresses that move you in a special kind of way. Mary can't reach out a hand and touch me in the way other folks normally communicate love and tenderness. In seeking to express her love, she had to find a substitute. Words wouldn't quite do it. They have their place, but it's not quite the same. What could she do instead to show that love? She developed two most effective ways to communicate.

She now has the most articulate eyes of anyone I know. Mary can speak worlds with a glance. She sends love messages to me that are beautiful and tender, and they so very adequately make up for the absent caresses.

And when she kisses me, it is an exciting moment! For she conveys more through the eager tenderness of her lips than many could with a passionate embrace. She is certainly not "handicapped" in this regard!

All that might be just the starry-eyed claim of a sentimental romantic except that these two techniques have been perfected by her only in very recent years of our marriage. How I appreciate and love her for working so hard with what she has to send her love responses to me, and I'm getting her message loud and clear.

That makes me want to work harder at expressing my love to her. I'm motivated to plan more carefully for a special "together time" or to think of a personal, intimate gift to please her. Each effort that one of us makes toward the goal of expressing mature love causes the other to want to respond in kind—and brings richness to both.

One day, another young couple came into my office asking to be married. Unlike most of the others, they had already been living together for some time. The young girl was obviously the one most urgently motivated to seek marriage.

When I questioned them about this desire, she hesitatingly responded, "Our relationship is neat, but it's so uncertain."

"You feel insecure in this arrangement of living together?" I asked.

"Yeah, I guess that's it," she said. "I want to know that we're playing for keeps—not just playing house."

That desire for more permanence in the relationship has been echoed scores of times in recent years by young women who have entered our pastoral offices of the church. They have found that the novelty of having a bed partner readily available in the same house is not all that they really wanted. Something was missing in that arrangement. They frequently confess to feeling "used" by their sex partners under these circumstances. Without any outside pressure or moralizing from anyone, they conclude that just living together isn't the right way to go. They realize that while they are giving themselves as mistress and housewife (there are inevitably the dirty socks and shorts to launder) and often working to contribute to the common income their roommate has no responsibility whatever to continue this living arrangement. The first day he tires of the whole thing, he can simply leave! When this awareness overtakes them, the girls start thinking of marriage. They want a greater commitment.

If they succeed in convincing their "roomy" to marry, it may be with the same reservations one such young man voiced to me. When asked if there were any changes he and his companion would like to make in the very traditional wedding ceremony I use, he responded, "Yes, there is something. You know where it says 'Till death do us part'? We'd like that to read, 'As long as the good we do for each other outweighs the bad.'"

"No way!" I exclaimed. "That's not a marriage at all! You're trying to leave the back door wide open so that at the first sign of difficulty you can split! You see," I continued, "it isn't the fancy words that the minister speaks in the ceremony that really bind a man and woman together. It's the *commitment* they make to each other, that they are willing to voluntarily and deliberately voice *before God and everybody*, that really is the essential ingredient of the marriage. Without commitment, there is no marriage."

Perhaps, the objective of true and lasting commitment is the highest goal of all in marriage. Like love, however, our commitment must be renewed constantly. It is made anew each time we *will* to act in a loving way—each time we *decide* to respond in a tender, loving manner to our mate. It is

Commitment is the adhesive that cements our relationship into something worthy to be called a marriage.

reborn with each victory over petty resentment and anger. It grows with vigor out of each resolution to "stick it out" when the going is tough. Commitment is the adhesive that cements our relationship into something worthy to be called a marriage. It is also the stuff that carries one through the perplexing stages in marriage and adult life, and there are plenty of those.

Frequently reaffirming that commitment has been a necessary part in the constantly growing experience of our marriage. As I have openly reaffirmed my commitment to Mary in any number of public situations, my love for her has grown and deepened. As she in turn has pledged her love to me in a hundred different ways in the presence of friends, loved ones, and God, my excitement over our relationship has increased, and her love for me has multiplied. For me, I suppose commitment comes down to deciding each day of my life that *I want to be married.* That requires a mature view of love and marriage. It's a comprehension that's built from the failures and successes, the disappointments and the achievements of twenty-six rich, eventful years. Great marriages like ours are not built on a "sometimes" love. Ours is a love that sticks. It's a love that takes the unexpected, the distasteful, even the hurtful, and turns it into steel-like fiber for endurance. It's a love that stubbornly refuses to die!

Would I do some things differently if I could go back and run the whole thing through again? Of course I would! Looking back, who couldn't see opportunity to spend more time together? Who wouldn't wish for greater communication? Who would be so blind as not to see in retrospect the too-frequent times of preoccupation, of neglect?

If I could start it all over from the beginning today, I would give my marriage the number one priority of my life. Nothing—not even my ministry—is of such limitless importance or of such inestimable value as my marriage to Mary!

It's not perfect yet, to be sure, but it's getting better all the time. And the quiet, unassuming woman who is developing her side of the marriage from a chrome-plated, four-wheeled chariot makes my life behind its wheels nothing less than sheer delight!

epilogue 2002

A good story has a way of wrapping its gentle fingers around your heart and mind and refusing to let go, and despite every intention to the contrary, one experiences a continuous tug to know the end of the tale. One is drawn with increasing, unremitting curiosity to learn the outcome of it all, and the conclusion leaves one with either a sense of completeness and fulfillment or perhaps of challenge. Usually, that is.

Sometimes, the story isn't yet finished. A life story may still be in process. That makes it all the more engaging, for one cannot possibly guess the direction it will take, or the outcome of the final chapter. That's why Mary's story continues to be so captivating.

All that Mary and I have learned about God's steadfast love has been confirmed over and again. As the southern gospel song aptly says, "God isn't good just some of the time—He's good all of the time!" His love is not conditional or sporadic. It is lavished upon His children every single day.

In the twenty plus years since the first appearance of this book, Mary's life story has unfolded along some unexpected lines. Each episode has shown her to be the unusual, really remarkable lady that she is. The passing years have naturally brought a growing number of events to be added to our album of memories. In common with the experience of most folks, some have been hilariously funny, some have been filled with excitement, and some have drawn tears to the eyes. In all, I have been reminded so many times of the incalculable gift of God in granting Mary's presence with me along the way. While earlier years convinced me that she was a most unusual lady, the following decades have opened my eyes and my heart to the endearing qualities that spell out her uniqueness.

Our children have grown to maturity, married, and had children of their own. Our daughter, Karen, graduated from Westmont College and afterward married the youngest son of our family physician. Scott Jacobs, her choice of a life partner, was the nicest thing that could have happened to her. Together, they have graced our lives with four wonderful grandchildren, each one bringing a special kind of joy and pride to adoring grandparents.

Only six months after Karen's wedding, our son Ken met his bride at the altar of an old but lovely Spanish-style chapel near our home. Kim, his bride, had been a part of our youth department at the church in Pomona. She has become the very capable mother of his two children, giving us a total of six grandchildren. What a delight and challenge these six are to the both of us.

Becoming a grandmother was one of life's happiest events for Mary. She radiates enthusiasm for the opportunities this provides to encourage and love these six grandchildren. She quickly outstripped her husband in developing these skills. For example, she began planning our summer vacation trips around the busy schedules of the grandchildren. In that manner, we could invite one or more of the children on each trip allowing them the opportunity to travel to many national parks, beaches, museums, forts, presidential libraries, and cultural, educational centers.

Mary exhibited such practical wisdom in the rearing of our children, so now she coaches me in the role of a grandparent. While I am sometimes overwhelmed by the grandchildren's music and fashions, I discover over and again the intensity of their commitment to what they believe. As these beliefs are molded and fashioned by life experience that is often difficult for them to accept and understand, I find golden opportunities to "come alongside." Not to lecture them about what they should do or how they should act, but just to listen. Maybe, that's the choicest of all the privileges of grandparenting.

Our church family has been continually gracious and loving to us. On our twenty-fifth wedding anniversary they sent us to Hawaii, and on our twenty-fifth anniversary as a member of the church staff they provided a cruise in the Caribbean. Later, they provided a cruise to Alaska. Their appreciation for Mary's ministry in the church has been well-demonstrated.

During the early years that Mary spent in tutoring, counseling, and teaching, recognition of her gifts quietly spread throughout the community. As her own church family took cognizance of these qualities, they began gently urging her into a leadership role in the ministry with women. It was an uneasy and hesitant process on Mary's part. As always, she struggled with the question, "Who will listen to an old lady in a wheelchair?" She was completely oblivious to the evident truth that literally hundreds of women all over Pomona Valley had already been listening quite intently to her words. It was simply astonishing to her that her life could produce such an impact on others, yet the writer of Proverbs reminds us, *"The reward of humility and the fear of the Lord are...honor and life." (Proverbs 22.4)*

Mary began cautiously assuming leadership in the church by inviting key women of the congregation into our home. Together, they have explored the felt needs of the women. As a pattern started to emerge from these group conversations, Mary envisioned the first of many endeavors to meet these needs for inspiration, fellowship and personal growth.

The first venture that developed came to be known as Joy Day. It was a very special day for the ladies that combined inspiration, instruction, and warm, friendly association. This involved the major portion of a Saturday once a year. It included a lovely luncheon served in the most refined and elegant manner in beautifully appointed surroundings. The very finest of feminine communicators in the country were engaged to share in workshops, plenary sessions, and at the luncheon. The popularity of this event grew rapidly and spawned other such efforts in sister churches in the region. Eventually, these churches began to send their Women's Ministry Coordinators to interview Mary.

It was a continuing concern of Mary's that women of the church needed programs of Bible study that were directed especially to their needs. Over the years, she has quietly prompted the Women's Ministry Committee to sponsor such programs as Bible Study Fellowship, Cornerstone Bible Studies, and Joy-In-Living Bible Study series. Each of these fine programs flourished among the hundreds of women of the congregation, meeting the desires for a certain style of study program. Throughout, however, was a persistent desire for a study led by "one of their own" women. Eventually, the Thursday night women's Bible study was initiated. Based on the Joy-in-Living study program from Oak View, California, Sheila Rapp, a deeply committed and gifted leader, who herself has completed many years of training and study in Bible Study Fellowship, led the group. Only God can assess the ultimate value of these several study programs that were the vision of the "lady in the chair."

Over the years, there have been any number of times that the circumstances of Mary's life have been severely trying, yet this unusual lady has maintained a steadiness that can only be understood in terms of the foundations of her life and faith. For Mary, trusting the Lord to meet her needs is a profoundly more courageous matter than most of us "unchallenged" folks can appreciate. To be sure, it is hard for someone who has functional arms and legs to understand what it is like to be without the use of either. Try as we might, the rest of us will miss a thousand little agonies that accompany the struggle to live a positive and productive life.

For the severely physically challenged, maintaining an adequate sense of self-worth is a daily and formidable obstacle. While others who have full use of their bodies and faculties exert natural control over their personal environment, the disabled person may be totally dependent upon someone else to manage that arena of life for him or her. The quadriplegic cannot easily adjust the thermostat or open and close the door. The difficulty of just performing simple, personal grooming and toileting routines can be immeasurable.

It is, therefore, really important that spouses and family members understand something of this "control thing." That is, the deep-seated need of the disabled to still have control over as many areas of their life as possible. It just may be that our sense of personhood is determined to some degree by our ability to control our environment, our circumstances, even our future. Ultimately, of course, that sense of being in control will come into conflict with some other people's efforts to maintain meaning in their own life.

However, there is a level of this "control thing" that can on occasion prove more complicated than what we have suggested here. It is a more intense or threatening sense of losing present control, especially in the area of relationships. Whether right or wrong, if the disabled person senses a diminished intimacy with a spouse, for example, there can be a surge of jealousy toward someone who is perceived as responsible for this change. Whether the spouse has unknowingly done anything to trigger this emotional upset is actually incidental. This sort of thing must, of course, be dealt with openly but gently, and whatever explanations are given need to be accompanied by physical touch to convey assurance. All of us, it has been noted, function best with at least one hug every day. There is something wrapped in a loving embrace that says, "You are worth everything to me. You are important!"

The truths that Jesus taught us more than four decades ago about relationships have not changed. They still work wonders in bringing love and harmony to the home. Recently, at our fiftieth wedding anniversary party, the impact of this was brought home dramatically as we listened to our two grown children speak. Karen spoke first:

"As your daughter, it seems most appropriate to say 'thank you' because your fifty years together bring such wealth to my own life. By your commitment to the vows you spoke to one another so many years ago, you have given me exquisite lessons in faithfulness, trust, humility, purity, integrity and diligence. By your example, you have taught me what it means to live out the marriage vows, not with a sense of drudgery or resignation but rather with faith, hope and love. You have given my life a solid foundation, by loving one another so well. Thank you.

In addition to the model I've had of marriage, you have given me an even greater gift—you taught me about a God of love, grace and mercy. Thank you for not being lukewarm about your faith. I am eternally grateful that God, in His mercy, chose to give me parents who are unafraid to proclaim and to live out their faith. Thank you for teaching me about God's love, the gift of His presence in my life, and His desire to walk with me through all of my life. You taught me who my rock is, where my strength comes from, and who it is that stands as my unshakable fortress. I have seen God's faithfulness at work in your lives, and so I have evidence to help me trust when clear vision has not been given.

I love you. I am blessed to be able to say that I respect and admire you as well. Thank you for living the life you have chosen to lead. Thank you for continuing to say 'yes' each time God asks, 'Are you willing?' I know He has mightily used you both in the lives of many people. And as your daughter, I know how well you have loved me, and how you opened my spirit to truth and life. So I celebrate with you, fifty years of marriage and ask that God grant you many years!"

Then, Ken spoke:

"'For a man shall leave his father and mother, and cling to his wife, and the two shall become as one.' God's command for marriage is for us to love and honor each other and to become more Christ-like in our lives and marriages. You have shown that these commands can be followed and obeyed, even when it's not fun or when you don't 'feel' like it.

Marriage is about commitment, an idea not very popular today. Mom and Dad, you have been committed to each other now for fifty years. You have followed the biblical principles that are intended to enrich marriage. You have been strong in the face of adversity, patient in the face of anger. Your example of marriage has been the shining light to many of us here today.

We want to say thank you for the courage, love, devotion, instruction and commitment your marriage has embodied for these past fifty years. Without that example, strength, counseling, and courage, some of us might not be where we are today. For me you are parents, counselors, mentors, and friends, and I want to say thank you.

To you, Mom, I want to say I love you. You've walked me through some hard times. You've rolled with me down the great times. You always have a soft word or biblical passage at just the right time. You've prayed me through good and bad. You are stronger than any ten men could hope to be. Thank you.

To you, Dad, thank you for the 'real' man that you are. The 'little man with the fuzz beneath his nose' is anything but little. If honor and integrity are true measures of manhood, you stand as the giant among us. You have lived the meaning of strength. You have taught me, by example, courage far beyond even Daniel's. You have taught me that patience and love are achieved by faith. Thank you.

Today, we have all come to celebrate with you for fifty years of being and living what you have professed is right. For living, as you taught us, God would have us live. For being, as husband and wife, what we all would like to be. Your marriage and your life together as man and wife have reached out and made our lives better. Thank you. We love you both."

It has now occurred to me that looking back over one's past is a little like reading a good book for the second time. While the plot is familiar and the characters already recognizable, reviewing and reliving the story still gives a warm satisfaction. So many reasons to give thanks to Him emerge from walking again the now familiar paths. Yes, the Holy Spirit and the principles of the Word of God still produce good fruit—even in our stumbling, feeble lives. Thank God, His is not a "sometimes love"!

endnotes

1. David Sibbald, "Robert Burns," critical analysis of "To A Louse" October 2001 available at www.tamoshanter.free-online.co.uk/louse.htm.

2. Dr. Paul Popenoe, *Marriage Before and After* (New York: Funk & Wagnalls Publishing Co., 1943).

3. Dr. Howard Clinebell, *The Intimate Marriage* (New York: Harper and Row Pubs., 1970) pp. 243–245.

4. Dorothy T. Samuel, *Fun and Games in Marriage* (Waco, Tx: Word Books, 1973).

5. Rollo May, *Love and Will* (New York: W. W. Norton, 1969), 170.

6. Romaldo and Walter Spalding, *The Writing Road to Reading* (New York: Wm. Morrow and Co., 1969).

7. Joyce Landorf, *Mourning Song* (ADA: Fleming H. Revell, Co. 1974).

8. Martha Snell Nicholson, *The Heart Held High* (Chicago, IL: Moody Press, 1954).

MUSIC

INVESTIGATE THE EVOLUTION OF AMERICAN SOUND

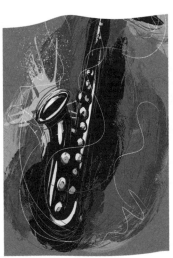

Donna Latham
Illustrated by
Bryan Stone

~ Titles in the *Inquire and Investigate* Series ~

Nomad Press
A division of Nomad Communications
10 9 8 7 6 5 4 3 2 1

This book was manufactured by Sheridan Books, Ann Arbor, MI USA.
November 2013, Job #352148
ISBN: 978-1-61930-203-7

Illustrations by Bryan Stone
Educational Consultant, Marla Conn

Questions regarding the ordering of this book should be addressed to

Nomad Press
2456 Christian St.
White River Junction, VT 05001
www.nomadpress.net

Contents

▾ TIMELINE

1607 ....Jamestown, Virginia, is settled by English colonists.

1619 ....African people are brought to Jamestown and sold into slavery. They share work songs and field hollers, relying on memory in the oral tradition.

1640 ....America's first book, The Bay Psalm Book is printed.

1700 ....Slaves sing songs based on old testament stories, reflecting their belief in Christianity.

1740 ....The Negro Act bans slaves from beating drums in South Carolina. They resist with the hand clapping and leg slapping of juba.

1775 ....The Revolutionary War begins. When British troops make fun of colonial fighters by singing "Yankee Doodle," Americans adopt it as their own.

1814 ....Francis Scott Key writes the poem "The Defense of Fort McHenry," which is renamed "The Star Spangled Banner." It later becomes America's national anthem.

1861 ....The Civil War begins. Julia Ward Howe writes "Battle Hymn of the Republic" after witnessing a skirmish.

1877 ....Thomas Edison invents the phonograph, a sound-recording device.

1913 ....*Billboard* magazine publishes a list of the most played vaudeville songs that are gaining popularity. This is a predecessor to their trademark Top 100 charts.

1917 ....America enters World War I. George M. Cohan composes "Over There."

1919 ....Chicago is established as the jazz capital with icons like Louis Armstrong performing in its clubs.

1923 ....The Charleston launches a national dance craze.

1925 ....Weekly radio broadcasts start at Grand Ole Opry in Nashville, Tennessee, featuring country and western music. Bessie Smith makes the first electronically recorded song "Cake Walking Babies."

1932 ....Vi-Vi Tone and Rickenbacker begin making and selling electric guitars.

1941 ....America enters WWII. People listen to the "Boogie Woogie Bugle Boy" on radios.

1945 ....American composer Aaron Copland wins the Pulitzer Prize in music for "Appalachian Spring," a ballet by Martha Graham that he composed in 1944.

1948 ....Long playing vinyl records are introduced by Columbia Records.

▾ AMERICA'S MUSICAL JOURNEY

1951 ....Jackie Brenston and his Delta Cats have the number one single on the *Billboard* R&B chart with "Rocket 88." Many consider "Rocket 88" as the first rock and roll record.

1954 ....Bill Haley and the Comets launch a frenzy with the huge hit "Rock Around the Clock." Elvis Presley becomes one of the first rock stars, with 60 million people watching him on the "Ed Sullivan Show."

1958 ....*Billboard* debuts its Hot 100 chart. Ricky Nelson's "Poor Little Fool" is the first No. 1 song.

1963 ....Bob Dylan popularizes protest songs. "Blowin' in the Wind" is sung at the March on Washington.

1964 ....The Beatles, a British band, gains popularity in America. This is the start of the "British Invasion."

1969 ....500,000 hippies and others swarm Woodstock for "Three Days of Peace, Love, and Music."

1973 ....DJ Kool Herc launches hip hop in the Bronx.

1979 ....The Sugar Hill Gang releases the first commercial rap hit "Rapper's Delight," popularizing hip hop nationwide.

1981 ....MTV debuts on August 1 with music videos geared toward adolescents.

1982 ....Michael Jackson releases "Thriller," the top-selling album in history.

1988 ....CDs outsell vinyl records for the first time.

2001 ....After 9/11 the current and former U.S. Presidents sing "Battle Hymn of the Republic" in the National Cathedral. America engages in war with Afghanistan.

2003 ....Apple iTunes Music Store is launched, allowing people to download songs for 99 cents.

2005 ....Pandora Radio, a web-based radio that personalizes its stations based on the listener's preferences, gains popularity.

2007 ....141 million iPods have been sold around the world.

2009 ....Pop icon Michael Jackson dies just before his comeback tour "This is It."

2010 ....Joan Baez sings "We Shall Overcome" for America's first African-American president, Barack Obama.

2012 ....The song "Gangnam Style" becomes the first YouTube video to surpass 1 billion views.

Introduction ▶

Make Your Own Kind of Music

How does music
inspire you?

 Music is an integral part of American history and heritage. It has the power to stir the soul and impact moods, to shape beliefs and motivate change.

What's on your playlist? Perhaps your taste in music is eclectic, with pop artists, R&B bands, and classic rock all providing the backbeat for your life. Do you download hip-hop tracks as soon as they drop, or scout old-school brick-and-mortar record shops for vintage vinyl? Maybe you make your own kind of music, belting out show tunes on karaoke machines, playing with your garage band, or guitar jamming with apps.

Music is inspirational. Have you ever wondered what's behind the music that moves you? Have you thought about the inspiration behind a popular song, whether it's indie or Top 40? Musical tastes are often deeply personal. You might love hip-hop while your brother only listens to jazz. But looking at musical trends offers surprising insights into a collective identity. Artists create music that reflects the time in which they live, with all its joy, strife, and messiness.

Social, political, and religious influences have shaped American sound from before we were a nation to the present. This same music helped form and empower an American identity, one with common core values that champion the individual, embrace freedom and democracy, and fight for civil rights. Within that collective identity is also the cherished right to protest and speak up—or sing out—against injustice.

RICH MUSICAL DIVERSITY

With its wide diversity of people and backgrounds, it's not surprising that the United States boasts an amazing array of musical influences from all over the world. From its earliest settlers, Americans discovered ways to weave Old World European traditions with new cultural influences to compose a unique identity.

The United States has contributed greatly to the world music scene, creating genres considered distinctly American. Its musical journey traveled from hymns and folk songs to patriotic tunes that fostered unity in wartime. It leapt from field hollers and soared on the wings of spirituals urging forbearance and spreading hope to those living in slavery. American sound be-bopped through jazz and the blues and throbbed into the rhythm of rock and hip-hop. And it rocks on!

ART AND SCIENCE

Music is both an art and a science. It's a constantly evolving creative expression that evokes strong emotional responses. Musicians are continually inspired by artists of the past, even as they find ways to add their own spins and create works that are uniquely their own.

There is a lot of new vocabulary in this book! Turn to the glossary in the back when you see a word you don't understand.

BLAST FROM THE PAST

In 2006, the popular TV show *Lost* featured the song "Make Your Own Kind of Music" by Barry Mann and Cynthia Weil. It's a golden oldie that champions individualism and urges singing your own special song. "Make Your Own Kind of Music" was a 1969 Top-40 hit for alto Cass Elliot (1941–1974). From 1965 until 1968, "Mama" Cass performed with Rock and Roll Hall of Famers the Mamas and the Papas, whose beautiful folk-pop harmonies rose from the Southern California music scene. After the band's bitter break-up, Elliot enjoyed a solo career until her death at age 32.

♪ **Evolving technology such as the phonograph, radio, iPod, and Internet have made music and its varied messages widely accessible.**

In *Music: Investigate the Evolution of American Sound*, you'll explore and analyze the history behind this popular art form. The activities in the book will introduce you to the physics of sound, music, and dance, as well as the physiology of hearing and singing. Like artists of the past and present, you'll apply what you discover to craft your own instruments, kick up your heels, write lyrics, compose music, and put on a show.

Adam Levine of the band Maroon 5 told *Vanity Fair* magazine, "The diversity in people's tastes is so much cooler. Everyone is saying MP3s and the Internet have ruined the music business and it's sad there are no more record stores—but music is so present now in the culture. More than it's ever been. That's a result of the technological advancements we've made."

We're fortunate to live in a time when we can access songs, music videos, TV appearances, movie clips, and recorded performances, even those produced decades ago. You can do this anytime, anywhere, with just the touch of a fingertip or a search on YouTube.

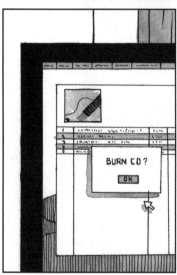

Chapter 1 ▶
Good
Vibrations

How do vibrations
create sound?

🎵 Acoustics is the scientific study of sound, which is a form of energy.

You usually know right away whether something sounds good to you or not. If you like a song you keep listening, if not, you change the station. What exactly is sound and why do we hear it?

VIBRATIONS IN THE AIR

When an object vibrates, it moves molecules in the air. These molecules bump into each other to make a sound wave. When waves of sound energy move away from the source of the vibrations and travel through a medium such as metal, water, or air, it causes a sensation in the ear. That sensation is sound.

Pitch is how high or low a sound is. If the vibrations are fast, the pitch is high. If they are slow, the sound is low. You've probably heard the siren of an ambulance blast shrill, high-pitched sounds to demand your attention. But foghorns, with their low-pitched blares, get your attention too.

Loudness and intensity affect the vibrations of sound. When you feel the floor tremble under your feet during a rock concert or feel bleachers rumble as a marching band leads its school team onto the field, you're experiencing loud, intense sounds with huge amounts of energy.

The loudness of sound is measured in a unit called a decibel (dB). Decibels are the force of sound waves against the ear. As sounds grow louder, decibels increase. A typical conversational tone you might use when chatting with a friend measures approximately 65 dB. If you yell across a room to get another friend's attention, that level increases to about 95 dB. If you have to raise your voice for someone else to hear you, you're at 85 dB or more. Long or repeated exposure to sounds above 85 dB can cause hearing loss.

THE HUMAN EAR

Your ear is extremely sensitive. How does it work? The pinna is the external portion of the ear that you can see. It captures sound waves and channels them to the external auditory canal. Sound waves move deeper to reach the tympanic membrane, typically called the eardrum. In the eardrum, the energy of sound waves transforms into sound. As the vibrations hit the eardrum, it flexes inward and outward. Sound waves vibrate the eardrum back and forth as the sensitive membrane detects the movement of molecules. The eardrum vibrates at a speed identical to the vibrations of sound.

MUSICAL NOTE

The decibel scale starts at zero. That's the weakest audible sound. A sound above 130 dB or more, such as a jet engine at 100 feet (about 30 meters), causes actual pain in your ear. And 160 dB will perforate your eardrum. A decibel is one-tenth of a bel, which was named after Alexander Graham Bell, who is known for inventing the telephone.

The vibrations of the eardrum move three tiny bones that press on the cochlea, a spiral structure that resembles a snail's shell. Tiny hairs in the cochlea respond to sound waves. Hairs at the front of the cochlea pick up high-pitched sounds. Deeper inside, longer hairs detect those that are low-pitched. These hairs send signals to the auditory nerve, which in turn sends signals to the brain. You perceive those signals as sound.

SOUND AND NOISE

What's the difference between sound and just plain noise? Noise is unwanted sound. Like musical tastes, this can be a personal distinction. One person's song is another's racket! Typically, sound is the sensation in your ear, while noise is an unexpected or unpleasant sound. When a pesky mosquito buzzes right next to your ear, it produces an annoying noise.

What's the difference between the sounds of music and noise? Music is arranged in regular patterns of pitch and rhythm. The sounds of noise are irregular and haphazard. But people can have strong opinions about music. Have your parents ever thought your music sounded like noise to them?

ARTISTIC MIX OF NOTES, PITCH, TONE, AND RHYTHM

When you hum along to the Beach Boys' "Good Vibrations" or a tune from your personal playlist, you're responding to music. Music is a creative, artistic arrangement of sounds—a pattern of vibrations in the air and a pattern or repetition of sounds. When you sing, you send sound vibrations into the air. How can you create vibrations with musical instruments? With a bow, you can release the rich, deep sound of a cello. You can pluck a guitar or other stringed instrument. You can toot a trombone or other brass, and wail on a reed to play the sax. Try clanking a cowbell or other percussive instrument.

Notes are arrangements of musical sounds in a specific order. In a standard scale, there are eight notes—A, B, C, D, E, F, G, A. To create music, a composer arranges notes in groups, called measures or bars. Pitch is a specific frequency of sound, how high or low a sound is on a scale. Each note on the scale represents a specific pitch. Tone is the quality of these notes. Some tones are called bright or dark, while others are warm or open.

MUSICAL NOTE

With their hit song "Good Vibrations," the Beach Boys added a new phrase to the vocabulary of popular culture. People started using the term "good vibes" to mean something that evokes a good feeling or positive energy.

With a classmate, parent, friend, or teacher, listen to the Beach Boys perform "Good Vibrations" with music by Brian Wilson and lyrics by Mike Love. Share responses to the song. Where do you notice complex vocal harmonies with backup singers singing different notes than the lead singer? Can you hear how the electro-theramin enhances the song? How does the song generate emotions that are simultaneously upbeat and melancholy?

 Rhythm patterns are the duration of and space between notes. These patterns provide the foundations of the different musical styles that you'll explore in this book.

Whether sung or played on an instrument, notes are held for a particular length of time. Music notation is a set of written symbols that specify the length and pitch of notes. We write notation from left to right in the way we jot words on paper.

Do you ever find yourself tapping your feet or bopping your head to a song? That's rhythm making you want to move. Rhythm is the pattern and emphasis of beats. Some beats may be stronger or longer or shorter or softer than others, but there's always a pattern of sounds and silences. Rhythm is the interval of measured time in a piece of music. But there's rhythm beyond music as well. In *Hearing and Writing Music: Professional Training for Today's Musician*, Ron Gorow writes, "Rhythm is everywhere: your breathing, pulse, the tides, days, seasons, life cycles, celestial motion."

FEEL THE BEAT

Until recently, researchers believed only humans could bop to different beats. But scientists recently revealed a sulphur-crested cockatoo named Snowball, who is a head-banging dancing machine! With synchronized moves, he grooves to his favorite song, "Everybody," by the Backstreet Boys.

Neurobiologist Aniruddh Patel received a viral video of Snowball bobbing, swaying, and stomping to "Everybody's" beat. Patel studies music and the brain at San Diego's Neurosciences Institute. Intrigued, he contacted Snowball's owner Irena Schultz, who lives in Indiana, and asked her to help him conduct an experiment.

His group took Snowball's favorite song and manipulated it on the computer, first slowing it down and then speeding it up. They asked Schulz to play the modified music for Snowball and videotape his reactions. The videos show that the bird will match his moves to the beat. For the slower versions, he swayed his entire body like a pendulum. But when the music got faster, he adjusted his movements to sway a little less and bob his head.

Adena Schachner, a graduate student in the psychology department of Harvard University, believes the parrot's dancing abilities may be linked to its capacity to mimic speech. Dancing may be a byproduct of vocal imitation and learning. To mimic a sound you have to listen to it and its rhythm. You have to use that information to coordinate the movement of your lips and tongue. Rock on, Snowball!

Notable Quotable

"I think there is something strangely musical about noise."

—Trent Reznor, songwriter, musician, and Academy Award–winning composer

PLAYLIST

View and listen to a video of Snowball's dance. Then turn down the sound and watch it again. Can you pick up the song's beat through Snowball's moves?

WARBLING WINEGLASSES

Ben Franklin was an inventor, composer, and musician who lived from 1706 to 1790. He created the glass armonica, which was a popular musical instrument of the time made of glasses mounted on a revolving spindle, played with a moistened fingertip. Where did Franklin find the inspiration for the glass armonica? At a musical performance in London, the performer's instruments were wineglasses of different sizes filled with water. With a wet fingertip, the musician circled the glasses' rims. The glasses responded to the friction in a variety of pitches, and the resulting vibrations produced ethereal, haunting sounds.

Work with your classmates, friends, or family members to create warbling wineglasses. Experiment with varying water levels to create different pitches.

🎵 The scientific method is the way that scientists ask questions and find answers.

Scientific Method Worksheet

Questions: What are we trying to find out? What problem are we trying to solve?

Equipment: What did we use?

Methods: What did we do?

Predictions: What do we think will happen?

Results: What happened and why?

- **Start a scientific method worksheet to organize your questions and predictions.** How will the amount of water in each glass impact pitch? How much friction will be required to produce vibrations and sounds? State your hypothesis. This is an unproven idea or prediction that tries to explain certain facts or observations.

- **Experiment by pouring different amounts of water into the different wineglasses to create an octave, or set of notes from A to A.** You can use the keyboard to establish the appropriate pitch for each note. Gently tap each glass with the spoon to test for a matching pitch. Is it easy to determine if the sounds are the same? How carefully do you need to listen? Does it help to have several people listen at the same time? How can you adjust the pitch in each glass so it matches?

- **Practice playing tunes on the glasses.** Start with something simple, such as "Happy Birthday." Don't get frustrated if it doesn't work right away. Make sure your finger is wet enough. Then, mix it up! Play more complicated but familiar pieces. See if others can identify them.

- **Work together to write a fantastical poem or story, and compose a musical piece that reflects the literary work's mood.** Ben Franklin penned a dramatic literary work to be performed with an accompanist on the glass armonica. Perform the work as someone accompanies you on the warbling wineglasses.

- **How accurate were your predictions?** How would you adjust your hypothesis? How did the musical accompaniment engage emotions or activate moods during the literary piece? Why do you think the glasses produce such otherworldly sounds?

Ideas for Supplies ▼

- science journal and pencil
- stemmed wineglasses of different sizes
- water
- metal spoon
- keyboard

To investigate more, search for an online performance of a street musician playing wineglasses. You might be lucky enough to watch one in person! What do you notice about their playing technique? Explore musician William Zeitler's glass armonica pieces with a family member or friend. What emotional responses do they ignite? Listen to Mozart's "Adagio and Rondo." These are delicate pieces he composed for the glass armonica. How do the pieces suit the instrument?

SPLISH, SPLASH

Vibrations that travel through air produce sound. These vibrations cause air molecules to move. They enter the ear, where we hear through air conductivity. Can sound pass through another medium? How will water impact the way sounds travel?

With a partner or group, first explore the way sounds travel through air, and then how sounds move in the water of a bathtub or swimming pool.

- **Start a scientific method worksheet to organize your questions and predictions.** How loud and intense will sounds be when they travel through air? Will the medium of water muffle or amplify sounds? Will it be easier to hear sounds in air or water? Discuss your ideas, and brainstorm additional questions. State a hypothesis.

MUSICAL NOTE

Sound travels more than four times faster in water than in air. Air conductivity and vibrations from our eardrum allow us to hear above water. When we're submerged under water, bones in our skull vibrate to hear. Bone conductivity is 40 percent less effective than air conductivity. Does this make it easier or harder to hear underwater?

- **In the air and in turn, smack together three sets of objects, such as those suggested.** Listen to their sounds. How loud and how intense are the sounds? Then, experiment in the bathtub or in a pool. Plug one ear and keep it above water. Submerge the other ear. Repeat the process, clacking each set of objects. Judge their loudness and intensity, and record your observations.

- **Assess your findings and draw conclusions.** Were your predicted results accurate? Does water muffle or amplify sounds? To analyze your data, try using computer software to generate a graph that illustrates the results of your experiment.

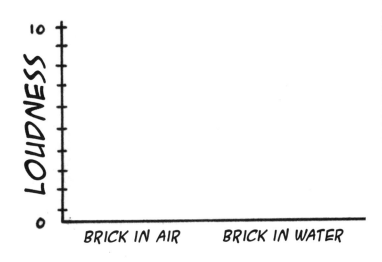

To investigate more, gather additional objects to test, or change the experiment's conditions. For example, what would happen if you plugged both ears during the water tests?

BLAST FROM THE PAST

With its wailing sax, honky-tonk piano, and joyful humor, "Splish Splash" was a 1958 breakout hit for Bobby Darin (1936–1973). Challenged to write a song that contained the line, "Splish, splash, I was takin' a bath," Darin dashed off the smash single. He claimed he composed the hit in 12 minutes! "Splish Splash" sold over a million copies and launched Darin's career as a rock and roll idol.

LISTEN UP! AUDITORY ACUITY

Auditory acuity is the keenness or sharpness of hearing. Acuity can vary with each of your ears, and it varies from person to person. Work with your teacher, a classmate, or a parent to investigate individual auditory acuity. Experiment with a subject's hearing as he or she covers each ear in turn and listens to sounds from a variety of distances and angles.

- **Start a scientific method worksheet and data chart to organize your questions, predictions, and data.** Share theories about how acuity will be impacted with distance and under different conditions. Discuss your ideas, and brainstorm questions. State a hypothesis.

- **With masking tape, make an X for the subject to stand on.** Mark a line on the floor 5 feet away (1½ meters) from the X and more lines every 5 feet. Note the distance on each piece of tape as you position it on the floor.

- science journal and pencil
- masking tape
- tape measure
- marker
- bell or chime

- **Ask the subject to stand on the X, and close his or her eyes tightly.** Have your subject cup a hand over each ear in turn. Ring a bell or chime from each distance marked. Can your subject identify where you are standing?

- **Experiment with producing sounds at different angles.** For example, raise your hands above your head to ring the bell, or lower them below your knees. How do these angles impact your subject's ability to identify the distance of the sound? Note all of your observations on the data chart.

Distance in Feet (Meters)	Sound's Angle	Right Ear Covered	Left Ear Covered
5 (1.5)			
10 (3)			
15 (4.5)			
20 (6.1)			
25 (7.6)			

To investigate more, switch places and have your subject test you to compare results. How can you create a spreadsheet or graph to present your findings? Analyze your results and assess your hypothesis.

PUMP UP THE VOLUME

Sound is a form of energy that travels in vibrations. The loudness of sound is measured in units called decibels, which is the force of sound waves against the ear. As sound grows louder, decibels increase. Work with others to experiment with different decibel levels. Experiment with decibels by creating a mini sound trampoline. Can we hear and see the sound?

- **Start a scientific method worksheet to organize your questions and predictions.** Do you think the vibrations of sound can physically move objects? How loud would it have to be? State your hypothesis.

- **Cover a bowl with plastic wrap to make a mini sound trampoline.** Place small pieces of dried pasta on top and set the trampoline on a speaker. What do you think will happen to the pasta when you play music?

- **Place the sound trampoline on top of a speaker.** Test different types of music, such as tunes with driving beats and pounding drums and those that are gentler. How does the pasta respond as you turn up the volume and increase decibel levels? Complete the data chart as you conduct your tests.

- **Work in groups to videotape the sound trampoline each time you test it.** Share your videotapes and compare the results. How do different pieces of music impact the pasta? With what piece of music do you observe the most noticeable responses?

Piece of Music	Volume Setting	Response of Object

To investigate more, test a variety of music genres. Make a new chart to track at what volume levels you prefer different songs. Do you notice that you prefer certain genres softer or louder than others? What about your favorite songs? Do you turn the volume up for songs you like better and down for songs you don't like as much?

Ideas for Supplies ▼

- science journal and pencil
- wide-mouthed bowl
- plastic wrap
- small dried pasta
- speaker
- variety of music
- data chart
- video recorder

Chapter 2 ▶
Colonial Times and the Music of Slave Life

How much did the slave trade influence American music?

🎵 Music gives us a chance to peek into the past to learn what people's lives were like, what they valued, and how they entertained themselves.

How have America's diverse music genres evolved? To understand American music, you have to go back to the very beginning, when the country was forming. Many of America's sounds have been influenced by the people held in slavery, whose roots were in Africa, and by the colonists who came from Europe.

Did you know that spirituals and folk songs inspired country music? Spirituals are religious songs—folk hymns based on stories in the Bible that were sung by slaves. Jazz, which originated in New Orleans, also evolved from slave music. Blues began with African-American traditions in the South, hopped the rails north, and became electrified in Chicago, where it maintains a strong identity. R&B, which combines jazz and blues, was rock's precursor. Even hip-hop's urban sounds trace their roots to Africa.

Colonial America was the time between 1607 and 1776, when people from Europe settled in colonies along the East Coast of what is now the United States of America. Let's see how America's diverse sound roots sprouted and took hold in colonial times, influenced by slavery, religion, and European tradition.

AMERICA'S FIRST SONGBOOK

When the group of colonists we now call Puritans left England to practice their religion freely, an ocean separated them from their homeland. But their songs came with them.

Twenty years after the Puritans and the rest of the Pilgrims first arrived in North America, the Massachusetts Bay Colony's first printer issued *The Whole Booke of Psalmes Faithfully Translated into English Metre* in 1640. Better known as *The Bay Psalm Book*, this was the first book ever printed in the New World. It was a pocket-sized translation of the Bible's Book of Psalms from Hebrew. *The Bay Psalm Book* was based on an earlier edition that colonists brought with them from England.

According to the Library of Congress, *The Bay Psalm Book* "represents what was most sacred to the Puritans—a faithful translation of God's Word, to be sung in worship by the entire congregation." This little songbook reflects the important values of political freedom and religious liberty on which the United States of America was founded.

🎵 The United States Library of Congress is the world's largest library, containing more than 144 million items. Among its treasure trove of rare books is one of 11 surviving copies of *The Bay Psalm Book*, now a piece of musical and political history.

Notable Quotable

"Music is an art of sounding, not writing."

—Richard Crawford, who wrote *America's Musical Life: A History*

🎵 **Folk songs are ordinary songs made up by ordinary people—regular folks. As the song changes over time, it becomes the creation of many people.**

ORAL TRADITION: FOLK MUSIC

What's the first thing you learned to sing? Maybe your parents sang the alphabet to you over and over again, or "Twinkle, Twinkle Little Star," and soon you were singing along. You were far too young to be reading the words. Long before MP3 devices, before CDs and albums, stereos and gramophones, even before the printing press and written language, people relied on a critical human technology—memory.

The New World's earliest European immigrants journeyed from the Netherlands, England, Scotland, and Ireland. They traveled with songs packed in the trunks of their hearts and minds. Immigrants spread emotional folk songs and ballads throughout Colonial America, which had been passed down from as early as the 1200s. Sharing by heart, people added special flourishes to make renditions distinctly their own. Stories and songs changed and evolved as they were told and retold, and sprinkled with inside jokes and personal commentary.

A folk song is any type of music that tells the story of what life was like in a certain time and culture. Traditional folk music came from farm and factory workers of the lower classes of the Old World. The original author is usually unknown and the songs are passed down orally and changed through families and other social groups.

The ballad is an important part of folk music. A ballad is a narrative verse set to song. It tells a poetic and melodramatic story, real or imagined, through short stanzas.

Many ballads tell tragic tales of murder or accidental death, and contain supernatural elements. Although ballads are packed with emotional power, their performers sing them with a calm voice to let the vivid words speak for themselves.

The tragic English love ballad "Barbara Allen" was first introduced in North America around 1666. Who first created the song? Centuries and generations later, it remains a mystery. The mournful song changed as artists tweaked details, invented character names, and made it their own. Some named characters after their own lost loves or set the tale in their own villages. Today there are at least 92 variations of "Barbara Allen."

HUMAN CARGO

The transatlantic slave trade formed the world's largest forced migration. From about 1500 to 1800, more than 10 million men, women, and children from West and Central Africa were enslaved. Through the slave trade, dealers transported people as human cargo to the Americas and sold them in the New World. Slaves labored in the fields of coffee, cotton, and tobacco plantations or worked inside homes.

Economic development in the New World depended on slave labor. Slaves formed the workforce. Many were experts at raising crops in tropical climates and at keeping cattle. Their agricultural know-how and hard work in the fields and in mines made their owners wealthy. Since slaves were considered property, they got nothing in return. They earned no wages, owned no land, and had no rights.

Notable Quotable

"Slaves sing most when they are most unhappy. The songs of the slave represent the sorrows of his heart; and he is relieved by them, only as an aching heart is relieved by its tears."

—Frederick Douglass, (1818–1895), an abolitionist who escaped from slavery and devoted his life to equality

SOUNDS OF SLAVERY

Because of Africa's enormous size, its people, and traditions are, and always have been, varied. Captured and taken from their homes all over Africa, the people forced to work as slaves in the Americas spoke many different languages. To communicate, they used a universal language—music.

Though cut off from their homelands, slaves kept their rich cultural identities and oral traditions alive. In Africa, music was the heartbeat of life. It expressed the feelings of entire communities. Slaves transported this importance of music to the New World. They sang frequently, expressing themselves by joining in sound and movement.

Forced to toil at backbreaking labor, slaves raised their voices in work songs and field hollers. Music relieved some of the drudgery of their repetitive work.

Many songs involved a call-and-response pattern with a caller, or leader, singing across a field of crops. A group sang out a chorus in response. With on-the-spot creativity, singers added unique touches. They embellished songs with quirky harmonies and tones. They synchronized the rhythm of their songs with their work, such as swinging axes, plucking cotton, and hoeing tobacco fields.

To replicate African instruments, slaves devised inventive uses for household items. Cider jugs became wind instruments. Spoons kept a percussive beat. From the dried and hollowed shells of calabashes, they crafted lute-like stringed instruments and percussive shakers.

African singing was totally new to European ears. The sound was much more nasal, loud, and shrill than what settlers were used to. The falsetto, shouts, groans, and deep rumblings were all sounds that were unique to African cultures. The bells, flutes, horns, marimbas, gourd shakers, and drums that ranged in size and sound were exotic instruments at the time. And the spontaneous and improvisational performance style of the slaves impressed Europeans.

SPIRITUALS

In spirituals, European hymns met with the African oral tradition to create a new American genre. As described by Soprano Randye Jones, "Spirituals are songs created by the Africans who were captured and brought to the United States to be sold into slavery. This stolen race was deprived of their languages, families, and culture; yet, their masters could not take away their music."

In the early years of the slave trade, African religious beliefs were extremely diverse. But music and dance were almost always features of their religious practices. Some colonists promised slaves freedom in exchange for converting to Christianity. Desperate for freedom, many slaves adopted the Christian religion of their masters, particularly the Baptist faith.

PLAYLIST

Listen to the work song "Hoe, Emma, Hoe." Evaluate the call-and-response pattern. How does the caller set up the song? How do responding voices add musical layers? Where can you hear embellishments and harmonies? Where do you think synchronized movements occurred as slaves worked the fields?

Hoe, Emma, Hoe, Anonymous

Caller: *Hoe, Emma, hoe, you turn around, dig a hole in the ground. Hoe, Emma, hoe.*

Chorus: *Hoe, Emma, hoe, you turn around, dig a hole in the ground. Hoe, Emma, hoe.*

Caller: *Emma, you from the country.*

Chorus

Caller: *Emma, help me to pull these weeds.*

Chorus

Caller: *Emma, work harder than two grown men.*

Chorus

Chorus

MUSICAL NOTE

The mournful spiritual "Go Down, Moses" illustrates a personal interpretation of the Old Testament's Book of Exodus 8:1. "And the Lord spoke unto Moses, Go unto Pharaoh, and say unto him, Thus saith the Lord, Let my people go, that they may serve me." The refrain, "let my people go," addressed the rebellion of Moses. He freed the Israelites from slavery and led them out of Egypt. But the spiritual also draws a parallel between the Exodus story and slavery. It expresses the struggle for freedom of enslaved Africans.

🎵 "Follow the Drinking Gourd" is written in a minor key to evoke mysterious feelings.

Even as they adopted Christian beliefs, enslaved Africans kept some of their own musical expressions alive. By about 1700, slaves were expressing their faith through song and traditional rhythms. Pounding broomsticks and stomping feet provided percussion. Chants and call-and-response lyrics were links to African forms. Even slaves denied the privilege of reading and writing could listen to, memorize, and retell Bible stories through powerful spirituals.

Spirituals were sacred folk songs shared in worship services. They contained complex layers of meaning. On the surface, spirituals retold Bible stories. Underneath though, they held deeper messages. They shared the sorrows and degradation of slave life and their inspirational lyrics urged hope and tolerance.

FOLLOW THE DRINKING GOURD

To express deep, hidden feelings of anger, fear, and a thirst for freedom, slaves relied on coded messages in the musical language of spirituals and folk songs. Some people believe "Follow the Drinking Gourd" contained secret messages hidden in its words.

These messages urged slaves to follow the Big Dipper north along the Underground Railroad. The metaphorical railroad was a secret network of safe houses. Abolitionists there assisted slaves escaping to freedom in the North.

How could a person fleeing at night find north? The fixed North Star in the night sky showed the way. It never changes position and always points north. Slaves were familiar with the Big Dipper and knew that two of its stars always pointed to the North Star. So by finding the Big Dipper, which resembles a giant, hollowed-out gourd, they could locate the pointer stars and head north.

In 1849, Harriet Tubman may have followed the drinking gourd to escape slavery in Maryland and flee to safety in Pennsylvania. She was the most famous conductor on the Underground Railroad, leading 70 slaves to freedom.

I SEE THE NORTH STAR. THIS WAY!

PATTIN' JUBA

After an uprising in 1739, the Negro Act of 1740 was a law passed in South Carolina to legally control the actions of slaves. They were not allowed to assemble in groups, raise food, earn money, or learn to read English. At the same time, some plantation owners banned slaves from beating drums. Owners feared slaves would use drumbeats to send secret codes over long distances and arrange uprisings.

But the ban couldn't stop the music. Slaves resisted and rebelled with creativity. Through juba dance, or "pattin' juba," they used their bodies as instruments. Briskly clapping their hands, slapping their legs and thighs, and tapping the ground with their feet, juba dancers created percussive sounds.

Irish and Scottish indentured laborers who stomped to lively fiddling influenced juba. Slaves may have imitated Irish jigs and step dances and Scottish clog dances. Over time, juba morphed into tap, a brisk, rhythmic, uniquely American form of step dance. All of these percussive forms influenced the "buck and wing" dance style, which is a lively solo tap dance with sharp foot accents, leg flings, and heel clicks.

William Henry Lane (1825–1852) popularized juba. Born free in Rhode Island, Lane combined patting juba with dances he learned from his Irish neighbor to create a new dance form. Using the stage name Master Juba, Lane played the tambourine and banjo and danced his way into huge popularity, performing in dance competitions all over the United States and for royalty in Europe. Lane is considered the inventor of tap dancing.

BEAT OF THE DRUM

In the United States, slaves maintained their African musical traditions and techniques while creatively adopting European styles and instruments. To keep time, many used juba and djembe drums, which they played with their hands instead of sticks. Traditional goblet djembe drums are constructed of wooden or clay bases with a drumhead of goat or other animal skin stretched across the top. A drumhead produces vibrations.

Work with your classmates or a group to construct drums from common household items, such as clay pots, deep metal bowls, and wide-brimmed plastic storage containers. Then investigate the types of sounds these different drums produce.

- **Start with some ideas and theories.** How will the size and shape of a hollow container impact sound? How does striking the drum in different places change vibrations and sound? How are powerful, resonant sounds produced? Discuss other questions with your group and formulate a hypothesis.

- **Make your drums and analyze their sounds.** Create a table to record the type of drum you are testing, what you strike it with, where you strike it, and the type of sound it makes. What happens when you strike different parts of the drumhead? Can you think of other ideas for drums now that you understand them better?

To investigate more, make more drums using your new knowledge. Play your drums to improvise along to some of your favorite tunes. If you make an MP3 recording you can share your drumming with others.

Ideas for Supplies ▼

- journal and pencil
- hollow containers such as clay pots and metal bowls
- drumhead materials such as plastic shrink-wrap insulating film, cloth, and cowhide
- string and rubberbands for insulating film
- scissors
- blow dryer
- objects to strike the drum
- audio recorder

MUSICAL NOTE

Through music, Native American cultures share oral narratives and histories. Drumming and percussive instruments, including rattles and bells, are important features of their musical traditions.

BECOME A BALLADEER

With the human technology of memory, balladeers learned stories, sprinkled on their own spicy flavorings, and spread ballads through oral tradition.

A ballad's rhyme scheme can vary. If it is a-b-a-b, the first and third lines and second and fourth lines rhyme, as in the first stanza of "Barbara Allen":

> *'Twas in the merry month of May (a)*
> *When green buds were a-swellin', (b)*
> *Sweet William on his deathbed lay (a)*
> *For the love of Barbara Allen. (b)*

If the rhyme scheme is a-b-c-b, the second and fourth lines rhyme, as in the second stanza of "Barbara Allen":

> *Slowly, slowly she got up, (a)*
> *And slowly she went nigh him, (b)*
> *And all she said when she got there, (c)*
> *"Young man, I think you're dyin'." (b)*

Swellin' and Allen and nigh him and dyin' are near rhymes—they don't exactly rhyme as May and lay do. The phrase merry month of May employs alliteration, which is repetition of like sounds at the beginnings of words.

- **With your classmates or friends, write and perform a four-verse ballad.** Ballads aren't always set to music, but they always tell a story.

- **Choose an incident from one of your favorite books to dramatize.** Select a scene that's thrilling and emotional, one that places the main character in a dangerous or difficult situation. Brainstorm ideas, and jot down notes.

PLAYLIST

Today, slow, romantic pop tunes, including Beyoncé's "Listen," Adele's "Someone Like You," Taylor Swift's "All Too Well," and Rihanna's "Diamonds" are called ballads.

- **Create a list of questions to consider. Decide on your rhyme scheme.** Will you use only exact rhymes or include near rhymes? Do you want to consider a refrain at the end of each verse? Will you set it to a familiar song, or recite it as a poem? Do you want to use musical instruments?

- **Rehearse your completed work and perform the ballad for others.** Ask your audience to share their responses. Challenge an audience member to recite part of the ballad. Did he or she recite it from memory or make changes?

> To investigate more, write another ballad with a different rhyme scheme. Change as many variables as you can think of. Record both your ballads and observe the differences.

♫ **Resonance is the sound a vibrating object produces.**

PLAYLIST

The spiritual "Lift Every Voice and Sing" is often called the African American national anthem. James W. Johnson wrote the inspirational poem in 1899. His brother John R. Johnson set it to music. View or listen to soul singer Ray Charles' gospel rendition and Wintley Phipps' booming baritone interpretation. Pay attention to how the different styles make you feel.

LIFT EVERY VOICE AND SING

How do we sing? The vocal cords are made up of two membranes stretched across the larynx. When air passes through the vocal cords, they vibrate. Sound resonates in the sinus cavities, throat, and chest, which are called resonators. The lips, tongue, teeth, and palate, known as articulators, work together to make the sound leave your body.

Investigate the vibrations of your resonators as you sing along with a recorded song or croon on your own.

* **Sing out loud! As you do, press your fingers gently against your throat and then against your sinuses.** Rest your palm lightly on your chest. Create a written list of questions to consider. Some ideas are:

   a. What do you feel?

   b. Can you feel vibrations anywhere else?

   c. Where are the vibrations strongest?

   d. Why do you think a particular resonator produces its specific vibrations?

- **Experiment with singing at different pitches, volumes, note lengths, and head positions.** Assess the different sounds you produce. Record your observations on the chart and analyze your findings.

Resonator	Pitch: Low vs. High	Volume: Soft vs. Loud	Length: Brief vs. Prolonged	Head Position: Straight vs. Tilted
throat				
sinuses				
chest				

To investigate more, try humming instead of singing, or explore the way your articulators respond to vibrations. Experiment with different types of songs, such as soft rock and loud, syncopated rap. How do they impact your results?

Lift Every Voice and Sing

Lift every voice and sing, till earth and Heaven ring,
Ring with the harmonies of liberty;
Let our rejoicing rise, high as the listening skies,
Let it resound loud as the rolling sea.
Sing a song full of the faith that the dark past has taught us,
Sing a song full of the hope that the present has brought us;
Facing the rising sun of our new day begun,
Let us march on till victory is won.

Ideas for Supplies ▼
- journal and pencil
- recorded songs
- data chart

A MAP TO FREEDOM

There were many escape routes out of the South, but the route detailed in "Follow the Drinking Gourd" is a famous one.

The song used code to tell slaves to follow the Tombigbee River, which runs through Mississippi and Alabama, to the Tennessee River. The Tennessee River runs through Alabama, Tennessee, and Kentucky. There, it flows into the Ohio River, a common escape route into the free state of Illinois.

- **Look at the explanation of the lyrics and refer to a United States map to follow the path.** Can you follow the trail?

- **Map out another route on the map. Write your own verses with coded geographical messages. Include a code-cracker to explain the messages.** Brainstorm creative, poetic ways to assign a second level of meaning to your lyrics.

MUSICAL NOTE

Have you ever told stories around a campfire? What made your story stand out? As stories and songs flow from one person to another through the oral tradition, original pieces change. People add in jokes and dramatic touches. A story with a grain of truth can evolve into one that's completely imaginative.

... THEN YOU JUST FOLLOW THE RIVER!

Lyrics	Coded Meaning
When the sun comes back,	Leave in spring when the days are getting longer.
and the first quail calls, follow the drinking gourd	Quail in Alabama start calling to each other in early to mid-April. Then find the Big Dipper and the North Star and head north.
The old man is a-waiting for to carry you to freedom if you follow the drinking gourd	"Ole man" is a sailing term for "Captain." This is said to refer to Peg Leg Joe who was once a sailor. Peg Leg Joe led many slaves to freedom.
The riverbank will make a very good road	Follow along the Tombigbee River out of Alabama.
The dead trees will show you the way Left foot, peg foot, traveling on, Follow the drinking gourd	According to H.B. Parks, Peg Leg Joe marked trees and other landmarks "with charcoal or mud in the outline of a human left foot and a round spot in place of the right foot."
The river ends between two hills, Follow the drinking gourd	The source of the Tombigbee River is near Woodall Mountain, the high point in Mississippi. There is a neighboring hill, but Woodall itself looks like two gentle hills.
There's another river on the other side, Follow the drinking gourd	The Tennessee River is on the other side. Following it north leads to the Ohio River border with Illinois.
Where the great big river meets the little river Follow the drinking gourd The old man is awaiting for to carry you to freedom If you follow the drinking gourd.	The Tennessee meets the "great" Ohio River in Paduchah, Kentucky. There you'll find Peg Leg Joe who will take you across to the free state of Illinois.

Ideas for Supplies ▼

- journal and pencil
- map of the United States
- colored pencils

To investigate more, use coded lyrics to create a route near your house or school. See if your friends or family can follow it! How will they know if they're on the right track? How do they know when they've arrived?

Chapter 3 ▶

The Birth of a New Nation: Patriotic Music

How did war influence American music?

 Patriotic songs like "Yankee Doodle" and "The Star-Spangled Banner" expressed common pride and hope for the future. They were also played for entertainment and to ease the burden on troops as they marched. Now these songs are part of our national heritage.

When the colonists declared their independence from England in 1776, the colonial period of American history ended. In the years leading up to the Revolutionary War, why did settlers in the colonies become so angry at the British government? Because the British made more and more laws to control the colonists and raise their taxes.

The colonists had no representation in their government. This means they could not vote for the people who governed them. The colonists had no way to influence their taxes or the decisions being made for them from across the ocean.

With the Tea Act of 1773, the government gave the British East India Company a monopoly on selling tea in the colonies. The colonists rebelled and a mob boarded three ships in Boston Harbor carrying East India Company tea. The mob dumped 342 crates of tea in the harbor in an incident that came to be known as the Boston Tea Party. More acts of rebellion followed and the colonists eventually went to war in a fight for independence.

"YANKEE DOODLE," 1760s

Do you know the words and the tune to "Yankee Doodle?" Like many kids growing up in America, you probably do. Kids all over the country sing, "I'm a Yankee Doodle dandy . . ." But what do these words really mean?

Like a lot of folk songs, "Yankee Doodle's" origins aren't totally clear. According to music tradition, a British army surgeon during the French and Indian War wrote the song to amuse a patient. He was making fun of the poorly trained and ill-equipped American colonists who fought with the British against the French over territory in Ohio and Canada.

Yankee was an insulting word for America's colonists. In the language of the day, *doodle* meant a foolish person and a *dandy* was used to describe a man overly focused on fancy clothes and hairstyles.

On the morning of April 19, 1775, British soldiers marched into battle in Lexington, Massachusetts, on the first day of the Revolutionary War. They sang the catchy tune and marched to its rhythm, teasing the colonial forces who they still viewed as unsophisticated and sloppy.

In June 1775, after the inexperienced colonial troops caused the British significant casualties in the Battle of Bunker Hill, the rebels took control of the cheerful song and turned it around. They wrote countless new verses that cleverly ridiculed the British. New lyrics praised their commander George Washington and encouraged pride and unity. The Americans were proud to be called Yankees, and "Yankee Doodle" became a patriotic song. Led by a corps of fife and drums, troops marched rhythmically along to their new rallying cry.

The harsh spirit of the Revolutionary War era produced "Yankee Doodle," which has become an American classic. Its beat made it a great marching song.

PLAYLIST

This is the first stanza and chorus of the original version of "Yankee Doodle." You can download a printable version of the full lyrics and the musical score from the Library of Congress.

Yankee Doodle

Father and I went down to camp,

Along with Captain Gooding,

There we see the men and boys,

As thick as hasty pudding.

Chorus

Yankee doodle keep it up,

Yankee doodle, dandy,

Mind the music and the step,

And with the girls be handy.

MUSICAL NOTE

British and colonial armies used fife and drum music to direct the movement of their soldiers. A company of about 100 men had one or two fifers and drummers. When eight or ten companies formed a regiment, the musicians formed a regimental band. The band used musical signals to position the troops onto and off of the battlefield and to change their formations, as well as to halt, march, or change their direction.

"THE STAR-SPANGLED BANNER," 1814

Peace did not last for long after the Revolutionary War ended and America gained its independence from Great Britain. America was a new country with new challenges and new allies. France had supported America during its war of independence, and many Americans felt that their new country should support France in its long war with Great Britain. As Britain continued to interfere in American's affairs, America finally declared war on the British Empire in 1812, beginning nearly three years of brutal battles.

Britain was determined to crush the rebellious Americans with an attack on Washington, DC, America's new capital. In August 1814, about 4,000 British troops set fire to the White House, the Library of Congress, the Capitol building, and other public buildings.

With the nation's capital in rubble, the British planned a double attack by land and water on Baltimore, Maryland, then the third-largest city in America. But after 24 hours of heavy attack, American forces defending Baltimore still held onto their city.

Lawyer and poet Francis Scott Key (1780–1843) was a prisoner on a British ship 8 miles away (13 kilometers). When he saw the American flag still flying the next day, he knew the Americans had not surrendered and Baltimore was saved. Deeply moved, Keys scrawled a poem on the back of a letter jammed in his pocket, which he called "The Defense of Fort McHenry."

A year later, Key set the poem to the tune of a popular British song. When the song was performed in public, the singer called the song, "The Star-Spangled Banner," and the title stuck. The honored song of loyalty and praise is an important symbol of an American identity and it officially became the national anthem through an act of Congress in 1931.

🎵 "The Star-Spangled Banner" is now played at events all over the country. You'll hear it before kids' sports games and Olympic competitions, on U.S. military bases at the beginning and end of each day, and at local festivals and community gatherings, especially on the Fourth of July.

OH! SAY DOES THAT STAR-SPANGLED BANNER YET WAVE...

"BATTLE HYMN OF THE REPUBLIC," 1862

During the 1800s, both the American flag and "The Star-Spangled Banner" were widespread symbols of patriotism. But the country was increasingly divided over the issue of slavery. As the United States expanded west of the original 13 colonies, there was constant disagreement over the spread of slavery to those areas.

Neither the North, whose people did not allow slavery, nor the South, whose people relied on slavery, wanted the balance shifted in the other side's favor. If more states forbade slavery than allowed it, the country might vote to end it everywhere. The South feared that their plantation economy of cotton and tobacco would collapse without the large, cheap labor force that slavery provided. The Civil War began in 1861 after South Carolina seceded from the Union. Several other southern states joined South Carolina to form the Confederate States of America.

During the Civil War, the song "John Brown's Body" became a popular marching song among Union troops from the North. Set to the tune of a popular church song ("Say, Brothers, Will You Meet Us?"), the song's lyrics tell the tragic tale of abolitionist John Brown. After leading 21 men on a raid to seize a government stash of weapons at Harper's Ferry, West Virginia, in 1859, Brown was put to death by hanging. He had planned to give the weapons to slaves to start a war in Virginia against slavery.

John Brown's body lies a-mouldering in the grave,

John Brown's body lies a-mouldering in the grave,

John Brown's body lies a-mouldering in the grave,

His soul is marching on!

How did this song become "Battle Hymn of the Republic?" In 1861, President Lincoln invited Julia Ward Howe, a poet and dedicated abolitionist, to visit Washington, DC. On a tour of Union army camps in neighboring Virginia, her carriage inched along roads clogged with marching soldiers singing "John Brown's Body." Civilians joined in, cheering the troops. Moved by the day's events, Howe was determined to write a poem more suited to the rousing music.

In 1862, *Atlantic Monthly* magazine published her poem, titled "Battle Hymn of the Republic." It became the anthem of the Union cause and remains one of the most cherished pieces of art produced during the Civil War. Its importance to America's identity and the fight against slavery remains today.

MINSTREL SHOWS AND VAUDEVILLE

Starting in the early 1840s and continuing through the Civil War era, popular entertainment reflected racist attitudes still prevailing in America. Minstrel shows featured white entertainers dressed as plantation slaves. They darkened their faces using burnt cork and imitated black musical and dance forms. Some of America's most famous songs, including "Oh Susanna" and "Camptown Races" came from minstrel shows.

After the Civil War, American society began to change. With a major move from rural to urban areas came a growing number of white-collar workers. This expanding middle class with steady earning power enjoyed more money and more free time to spend it. Vaudeville leapt onto the stage as a spectacular way to do both and it reigned as the most popular form of family entertainment through the early 1900s. Shows were part-theater, part-circus, and part-joke-o-rama.

PLAYLIST

View and listen to Julia Ward Howe's complete lyrics of the "Battle Hymn of the Republic." The first stanza and the chorus are what people hear most often. Why do you think the tune has lasted and been so popular for over 150 years?

Minstrel shows frequently included the same stereotypical characters. These included Jim Crow as a carefree slave, Mr. Tambo as a joyous musician, and Zip Coon as a free black man attempting to be from an upper class. Minstrel shows portrayed black people as lazy, simple, not very smart, and happy to be slaves.

Vaudeville offered a variety of short stage acts that ranged from mesmerizing Shakespearean actors to heart-stopping daredevil acrobats. Singers, dancers, jugglers, comedians, and animal acts promised something for everyone. People flocked to the shows. Whether they luxuriated in velvet cushions at vaudeville palaces, or squished together on wooden riverboat seats, audiences went crazy for the shared experience.

At home during this time, families gathered around the piano to sing popular songs such as "Daisy Bell" and "In the Good Old Summertime." As advances in printing made it cheaper to print sheet music, publishers issued vast amounts of parlor music, often with elaborate covers that illustrated popular culture. Sheet music became a perfect place for American companies to advertise their products. The margins of sheet music were even used during World War I to promote the war effort. "Food will win the war. Don't waste it!" appeared on sheet music published by Jos. W. Stern.

WORLD WAR I, 1914–1918

For much of World War I, America stayed on the sidelines while France, Russia, and Great Britain fought against Germany. But on April 6, 1917, the United States finally declared war against Germany and entered the conflict. World War I was largely a series of land battles fought from trenches. But advances in technology turned the battle into what is considered the first "modern" war. The catastrophic might of chemical weapons, massive tanks, and machine guns killed millions worldwide.

Some music of the era expressed unity and patriotism. On the day the United States entered World War I, George M. Cohan composed "Over There," which became one of the most famous songs of the war. On his way to work, Cohan couldn't help but notice newspaper headlines bursting with the announcement of America's involvement in the war. With a spark of inspiration, he created the rallying chorus,

O-ver there, o-ver there

Send the word, send the word, o-ver there

That the Yanks are com-ing, the Yanks are com-ing

The drums rum-tum-ming ev'-ry where.

By the time Cohan arrived at work, he had the verses, the chorus, the tune, and the title. The song sold more than two million copies before the end of the war and earned Cohan a Congressional Gold Medal.

But not everyone supported the war effort and there were many artists and performers who expressed this sentiment. In fact, the first big hit of the war, Alfred Bryan's and Al Piantadosi's "I Didn't Raise My Boy to Be a Soldier," spoke of widespread American skepticism about joining the war. Its mournful chorus sang of a mother's sorrow:

I didn't raise my boy to be a soldier

I brought him up to be my pride and joy.

The song humanized the enemy "over there" with the following lyrics,

Who dares to put a musket on his shoulder

To shoot some other mother's darling boy?

BLAST FROM THE PAST

In 1913, with World War I looming, George Gershwin (1898–1937) landed his first job in the music industry. He was only 15 years old! It was the start of a brilliant career that eventually made him one of the most sought-after musical composers in America. In an era before new recordings were widely available and sheet music was downloadable, music stores employed songpluggers to perform and promote sheet music. Pluggers like Gershwin sat playing new music at a piano positioned in an in-store balcony, giving shoppers a chance to sample the sounds before making a purchase. How does this compare to the way you can sample music before you buy it?

"GIMME FIFE!"

The fife is a wind instrument related to the flute and recorder. A wind instrument is a resonator—the tube—where a column of air vibrates when the player blows into or over the mouthpiece. The length of the tube and the way the vibrating column of air is changed determine the pitch of the sound. In medieval Europe the fife was used to play folk music for dancing.

The Revolutionary War period featured the fife played in the key of B flat or C. At the time, fifes were made from wood such as maple, walnut, cherry, cocuswood, and boxwood. Explore the sounds you can produce with a homemade flute, experimenting with posture, breathing, mouth positions, and finger positions.

- **Before you begin construction, sketch a design plan.** Indicate hole placement and measurements for spacing. What materials can you use? How long do you want your flute to be? How will you make the cuts for finger holes sharply defined? You will need to cut an embouchure hole in one end. This is the hole you'll blow into.

- **Build your flute according to your design.** The finger holes should not be ragged or too large to be covered by your fingers. The end of the flute with the embouchure needs to be plugged with a stopper to complete the flute. This way air cannot escape from both ends.

- **Holding a flute and using the embouchure hole can be tricky.** Musicians hold flutes horizontally to the right. They position the left hand with fingers curved toward themselves and knuckles away. One finger hovers over each of the three finger holes. The thumb rests beneath the instrument. Flutists position the right hand with fingers curved away and knuckles inward. With the thumb resting beneath the flute, three fingers poise above the remaining holes. Practice holding your flute. Try to keep your head upright and your arms relaxed. Are you comfortable? Check out your form in the mirror!

- **To produce sounds, flutists direct their breath into the embouchure hole.** They release breath from the lungs and through the position of the lips. With a relaxed face, they control only lip muscles. To try it out, purse your lip muscles over the hole. Blow a tight, quick stream of air across the opening. How can you make the clearest sound? How can you change the sounds you make?

To investigate more, design and construct flutes with other materials, such as bamboo or PVC pipe. How do the sounds you produce differ and compare? Can you teach yourself to play "Yankee Doodle?"

Ideas for Supplies ▼

- journal and pencil
- ruler
- scissors
- tube for the body of the instrument
- letter opener, screwdriver, or pen
- a stopper such as a plastic cap, cork, or cardboard circle

OH, SAY, CAN YOU SING?

"The Star-Spangled Banner" is one of the most challenging songs to sing, even for highly accomplished pros! The song requires a wide vocal range. It begins at the lowest range of the voice and soars to the highest. The song's low and high notes can be tough to reach. On top of that, its complex lyrics are easy to get wrong. Give the anthem your own spin!

- **Work with your teacher, classmates, or parent to explore different renditions of the national anthem.** Use your discoveries to arrange your own piece. Brainstorm some features to observe.

- **Note your observations and share your comments as you:**

  - View singer Whitney Houston's emotional solo at the 1991 Super Bowl. Many consider Houston's the definitive performance. How does she create a powerful delivery?

  - Compare Houston's performance with Alicia Keys's R&B interpretation at the 2013 Super Bowl.

  - Watch the a cappella performance of singer-songwriter Christina Aguilera at the 2011 Super Bowl. Even the talented, multiple Grammy winner missed some of the tricky lyrics. Can you hear where Aguilera accidentally sang, "What so proudly we watched at the twilight's last gleaming," instead of, "O'er the ramparts we watched, were so gallantly streaming"?

MUSICAL NOTE

In 2000, before she became one of the world's most successful pop-country artists, Taylor Swift (1989—) sang the national anthem for 20,000 basketball fans at a Philadelphia 76ers game. She was 11 years old!

- journal and pencil
- computer
- keyboard or musical instruments

- View Beyoncé's lip-synched rendition at President Obama's 2013 inaugural ceremony. Most people praised the moving performance but some critics felt the singer shouldn't have relied on a pre-recorded piece. The recording did guarantee a flawless performance during a solemn occasion in front of a global audience. What are the positive and negative points of lip-synching?

- Check out the dramatic, electric-guitar instrumental of Jimi Hendrix at Woodstock in 1969. How does it compare to vocal versions? How does drumming add impact?

To investigate more, think about which rendition most resonated with you and why. Which features influenced your opinions? Share your ideas. Then use those musical influences to arrange your own musical or instrumental performance of the national anthem.

The Star-Spangled Banner

Oh, say can you see by the dawn's early light

What so proudly we hailed at the twilight's last gleaming?

Whose broad stripes and bright stars thru the perilous fight,

O'er the ramparts we watched were so gallantly streaming?

And the rocket's red glare, the bombs bursting in air,

Gave proof through the night that our flag was still there.

Oh, say does that star-spangled banner yet wave

O'er the land of the free and the home of the brave?

JUG BAND ACOUSTICS

The music of jug bands evolved from African-American vaudeville performers in the South's urban areas, such as Memphis, Tennessee. Bands employed homemade instruments such as stoneware jugs played like wind instruments, metal spoons, comb kazoos, washboards, and gourd guitars. Mingled with traditional banjos and guitars, the energetic jug bands in the early 1900s were forerunners of the blues.

To play a traditional wind instrument like a trumpet or trombone, musicians blow air through their closed lips into a mouthpiece. Inside the instrument, air vibrates and shoots as a column into the resonator. The bell-shaped part at the front of the trumpet releases the sound as a musical note. By buzzing their lips across the rim of an open jug, musicians produce a variety of sounds.

MUSICAL NOTE

Contemporary jug bands perform toe-tapping country music using a wide variety of homemade instruments made from items found around the house.

Ideas for Supplies ▼

- journal and pencil
- empty soda bottles
- water
- spoon

- **Investigate the physics of jug instruments.** Create your own jug instruments using soda bottles and water. Brainstorm some ideas. How will water levels in soda bottles impact the pitch and tone of the sound you make? Write out your theories.

- **Discover what kinds of tones and pitches you can produce by blowing into the bottles.** Can you play a song? What happens when you rap the bottles with a spoon? How does the sound change? What if you leave one empty?

- **If you play a brass instrument, you're already adept at creating sound with the embouchure.** Brass musicians alter lip tension and airflow to produce different sounds. Predict how you can apply the same technique to produce sounds on an empty bottle. Formulate a hypothesis and test it out. What about trying out different methods of buzzing your lips across the bottle's rim. Which positions result in higher and lower pitches? Can you play a song?

- **Demonstrate your jug-playing technique for a classmate, teacher, or family member.** Explain the physics of your sound production.

To investigate more, conduct your experiment with a stoneware or glass jug, such as an empty cider or milk jug. How do your results differ? Apply what you discovered in Warbling Wineglasses when you experimented with varying water levels to produce sounds of different pitches.

Chapter 4

The Roaring Twenties: Jazz, Blues, and Country

How did the growth of American cities influence music?

Some people objected to jazz as vulgar and inviting sinful behavior. But many young people in the nation's big cities loved the wild music and dancing that came with this exciting new American art form.

After the bloodshed of World War I, Americans entered an era of prosperity, artistic innovation, and fast living that came to be known as the Roaring Twenties. For the first time, there were more Americans living in cities than on farms. Unprecedented industrial growth and the large-scale availability of electricity, cars, telephones, radios, motion pictures, and a vast range of other new products doubled the total wealth in America during this time. The war was over, people had money in their pockets, and it was time for fun. And lots and lots of jazz.

The first commercial radio station hit the airways out of Pittsburg in 1920. Just three years later there were more than 500 stations in America and radios in more than 12 million homes. People were listening to music from their homes all across the country. In 1927, people bought 100 million phonograph records, which they played on crank-up Victrolas.

As people moved from the South to the industrial cities of the North, they brought along traditions of blues and jazz that originated in the fields of the Mississippi Delta and New Orleans. In an era of segregation, these historically African American music styles became mainstream, making music a powerful tool in the struggle against inequality.

BIRTH OF THE BLUES

When we think of the blues, we think of feeling down. Blues music deals with feelings of loss, misfortune, and grief, but at the same time it is about having fun and letting our troubles go. It shows us how to find joy in sadness and shed the blues.

From the end of the Civil War through the 1940s, many poor people in the South, both black and white, worked in fields as sharecroppers. Some sharecroppers were former slaves working land owned by their former masters. They put in long hours and barely made a living after paying their landlords for food, housing, and farm supplies.

By the 1920s, sharecroppers had developed their own rural field music that evolved from the field hollers, ballads, and work songs of slavery. All along the Mississippi River Delta, sharecroppers mingled on their front porches at night after a hard day's work. They held fiddle contests, played music, and tapped out juba rhythms on their bodies. Most were illiterate and could not read music, so they used verbal and musical improvisation. As they shared personal stories of hardship, lost loves, and social injustice, the music helped them to beat the blues and feel uplifted.

PLAYLIST

Listen to Bessie Smith's "Thinking Blues." Notice the relationship between sound and silence in the song. There's "space" for call-and-response and other improvisational flourishes!

Notable Quotable

"New Orleans had a great tradition of celebration. Opera, military marching bands, folk music, blues, different types of church music, ragtime, echoes of traditional African drumming, and all of the dance styles that went with this music could be heard and seen throughout the city. When all of these kinds of music blended into one, jazz was born."

—Wynton Marsalis, jazz musician

MUSICAL NOTE

A flapper was a young woman in the 1920s who rebelled against the norms of the older generation. She wore short, bobbed hair and makeup, smoked cigarettes in public, and wore short skirts to dance to the energetic music of the Jazz Age.

The rhythms of the blues were taken from African drumming and played on guitar, banjo, harmonica, and later piano, sax, and trumpet. Musicians used their guitars to imitate human wails and shrieks. Together with moans, grunts, hollers, and other vocalizations, this created the sorrowful sounds that sparked the birth of the blues.

ALL THAT JAZZ

The lively sounds of jazz music that we know today emerged from the struggles of former slaves living in New Orleans. New Orleans style, or "Classic Jazz" started in the late 1800s and early 1900s with brass bands performing for parties and dances. Many of the musical instruments were salvaged from the Civil War, including the clarinet, saxophone, cornet, trombone, tuba, banjo, bass, guitar, and drums. It was a lively combination of ragtime, spirituals, marching tunes, and strong influences from the blues.

The earliest jazz musicians from New Orleans are not well known today. But when gravel-voiced Louis Armstrong (1901–1971) was discovered and first went to play in Chicago in 1922, jazz took off. His music was a collection of improvised solos around a structure. Improvisation is central to all jazz music, even when a musician is playing from printed music. A jazz tune might start out sounding like a slow, introspective blues song, but would then take off in unpredictable directions as musicians improvised and turned it into something entirely new.

JAZZ AND BLUES ON THE MOVE

Jazz and blues musicians flooded Chicago, Detroit, and other cities to escape segregation. For musicians heading north, Memphis, Tennessee, was an important stop along the Mississippi River. Blues musicians such as Memphis Minnie and Bessie Smith (1894–1937), the "Empress of the Blues," played to packed crowds at theaters on Beale Street in Memphis. By the end of the 1920s, Smith was the highest-paid black entertainer in the country, playing in sell-out theaters throughout the South, the North, and the Midwest.

Born McKinley Morganfield in Rolling Fork, Mississippi, Muddy Waters (1913–1983) grew up playing the blues harmonica and guitar in the swampy puddles of the Mississippi River. He eventually joined a traveling show and gained recognition.

Muddy Waters moved to Chicago in 1943 where he began playing in clubs and developed a style that gave an urban vibe to the rural Mississippi Delta blues. His hit single "Rollin' Stone" influenced the name of the major music magazine *Rolling Stone* and the famous rock band, the Rolling Stones. The electric blues sound of Muddy Waters made its way to England, and he became an international star who recorded with rock musicians well into the 1970s.

🎵 The blues flourished in Chicago with Muddy Waters, who is called the father of modern Chicago blues.

In Chicago, Louis Armstrong introduced the art of wordless, nonsense improvisation known as scat singing. Other bands from New Orleans made their way north and jazz spread to Europe as African American musicians flocked to Paris in search of cultural and creative freedoms.

Jazz became so popular in the 1920s that roadhouses filled with people kicking up their heels to its spontaneous sounds. They flocked to dance halls to hear jazz musicians and their big band orchestras. The Benny Goodman Orchestra at the Savoy in New York City and Duke Ellington at the Aragon in Chicago were sometimes joined by blues great Bessie Smith. Flappers danced new dances with names like the Black Bottom, Flea Hop, Cake Walk, and Charleston to the music of the big bands.

At the end of the decade, jazz began to take on a more free-flowing rhythm that became the trademark of the swing style of jazz. Early swing bands could have 16 or more instruments playing with and against each other. Hot bands like Count Basie's played quick, hard-driving tunes. Others like the Glen Miller Orchestra played slower, less improvised heartfelt songs. By the 1940s, solos were popular and band leaders became part of the orchestra, playing an instrument instead of conducting from the front. Dancers loved this music and a new swing style of dancing evolved.

COUNTRY AND WESTERN MUSIC

With chart-topping bands and artists including Lady Antebellum, Taylor Swift, Carrie Underwood, Garth Brooks, and Tim McGraw, country music enjoys a huge following. Like folk music and the blues, country is all about storytelling.

Country music evolved from European fiddling and African banjo playing, but it wasn't until the 1920s that country music took hold as a new genre of American music. Irish immigrants were among the first Europeans to settle in the southern Appalachian Mountains. Along with their beloved folk songs and ballads, the Irish brought their fiddles! This versatile instrument can swing from bouncy to melancholy. It inspires a range of emotions and was perfect for joyful jigs and reels as well as weepy ballads. People kicked up their heels to the fiddle's lively tunes and swayed to sorrowful ones.

The gourd banjos brought to the New World by slaves also inspired country music. African musicians covered bowl-like gourds with heads made from taut animal skin. Animal hair and plant fibers made heavy strings. These instruments probably produced low, mellow sounds. White folks in the South modified the instruments by crafting wooden banjos covered with groundhog-skin heads. By the mid-1800s, people played their fiddles and banjos together, laying the roots for country music and its offshoots.

In the early 1920s, artists like Fiddlin' John Carson, the Skillet Lickers, and Vernon Dalhart recorded some of country's first hits. WSN Radio's Grand Ole Opry began broadcasting live country music acts from Nashville, Tennessee, every Saturday night over the radio. And when Victor Records signed a recording contract with Mississippi native Jimmie Rogers in 1927, he became a major star with his release of "Blue Yodel #1," which sold over a million copies.

🎵 **Fiddle music was once called Old Time Music. As it developed into what we now call country and western, the genre kept its rural down-home sounds.**

MUSICAL NOTE

In 1925, Nashville's Grand Old Opry began weekly broadcasts of country music. With bluegrass, gospel, folk acts, and silly skits, the legendary show continues its run today. It has been instrumental in promoting country music artists ever since. You can listen to a live stream at www.opry.com/wsm/

🎵 **Because country music was often played on the same radio station as cowboy music, the term "country and western music" evolved.**

PLAYLIST

Listen to songs from several categories to experience the genre's different spins. Explore music from well-known country artists of the past and present.

bluegrass: Alison Kraus, Jimmy Martin, Dolly Parton, Earl Scruggs, Nitty Gritty Dirt Band

country and western: Hank Williams, Patsy Cline, Merle Haggard, Taylor Swift, Garth Brooks, Tim McGraw

cowboy: Gene Autry, Roy Rogers, Sons of the Pioneers

honky-tonk: Lefty Frizzell, Webb Pierce, Stonewall Jackson, Wanda Jackson

MUSICAL NOTE

Patsy Montana and her hit, "I Want to be a Cowboy's Sweetheart," led the way for women to have their own solo careers. Later many female Nashville Sound country artists recorded big hits, including Patsy Cline, Kitty Wells, Brenda Lee, and Loretta Lynn.

COWBOY MUSIC, BLUEGRASS, HONKY TONK, AND THE NASHVILLE SOUND

In the 1930s and '40s, cowboy movies popularized country music, which was sometimes called western music. People flocked to the movies to watch singing cowboy flicks on the big screen. Artists including Gene Autry, Roy Rogers, and Dale Evans crooned in clear, light tenor voices about life on the open range out West. String bands and harmonicas accompanied songs such as the Sons of the Pioneers's "Tumbling Tumble Weeds" and Gene Autry's "Cowboy Blues."

At the same time, Bill Monroe, Lester Flatt, and Earl Scruggs were spearheading the growth of bluegrass. This branch of country is known for its high, lonesome sound. Blended with English, Irish, Scottish, and Welsh traditional music and jazzy African-American flavors, bluegrass is infused with the sounds of stringed instruments. Like all other folk music, bluegrass rings with the spirit of the working class. Tunes such as "All Aboard" and "John Henry" told tales of hardscrabble times in railroad towns. "Sprinkle Coal Dust on My Grave" and "Dark as a Dungeon" lamented the treacherous jobs of Appalachian coal miners.

The 1950s brought another style of country music known as honky-tonk. At the time, a honky tonk was a bar located in a rural white southern community where people went to escape their difficult lives for a little while with live music. Sometimes called hillbilly, honky-tonk music embodies a spirit of working-class life, loneliness, drinking, and lost loves. Honky-tonk had its roots in the western swing style of country combined with jazz. The fiddle and the steel guitar feature in most of the songs, with stars such as Hank Williams, Lefty Frizzell, and Ernest Tubb.

In the late 1950s and '60s, a new country-pop Nashville Sound gained a large following, putting an end to the reign of honky-tonk. Nashville Sound combined country with the smooth sounds of popular jazz and swing bands of the day. Jim Reeves, Patsy Cline, and Eddy Arnold were the emotional, expressive crooners who brought this new, easy-listening country sound to larger audiences. They cemented country and western's place in American sound.

BLAST FROM THE PAST

Music has always brought people together. Bluegrass bands allowed folks to hang out and enjoy the music—and jump in for foot-stomping good times. Families and friends gathered on front porches and in homes. They stomped percussive Celtic clog dances. Watch these vintage clips. Take a look at the kids' vigorous clog dancing at a house party. Listen for the bouncy fiddle and bright banjo. Watch the Blue Ridge Mountain Dancers perform with Pete Seeger. Can you hear the buoyant fiddle and twangy banjo?

PICK A SOUND

Bluegrass music gets its distinctive sound from stringed instruments. Bluegrass musicians play fiddles, resonator guitars, upright basses, mandolins, and banjos. Stringed instruments produce sounds through the vibrations of strings in tension. The thickness and length of the strings determine the types of sounds produced. For example, a thin string produces a higher sound than a thick one. A loose string produces a lower sound than a tight one. How do different methods of playing impact sound?

Explore the way the sounds produced with the downward clawhammer style differ from the upward Scruggs style.

MUSICAL NOTE

The clawhammer is the oldest playing style. Slaves introduced this traditional style without picks, which many musicians use today.

- **First test out the clawhammer style.** Cup your hand like a claw against the banjo strings. Position all your fingers together. Keep the thumb separate, raised a bit above your fingers. Your hand will move in a downward direction. With a downstroke, strum a string, or strings, with your index and middle fingernails. Your thumb should catch strings, too. Experiment with the clawhammer until you feel comfortable with the style. Watch the way the strings vibrate as you strum down.

- **Now try the Scruggs style.** Slip on the thumb pick and cover your index and middle fingers with picks. Let your ring finger and pinky rest against the banjo head. Pluck upwards with the picks. The motion can be tricky. It requires dexterity.

- **Experiment with the Scruggs style until you are comfortable.** Some people find fingerpicks awkward. It might take extra practice to feel at ease. How do the strings vibrate as you play?

- **Record yourself playing a song or just noodling with both methods.** Listen to your recordings, and discuss your observations. How would you describe the sounds produced? How are they similar and different? Why do you think the two methods produce different sounds? What conclusions do you draw?

To investigate more, use a flat pick to play the banjo. What differences do you hear in the sounds you produce? Why do you think they are different? Now use all of the styles you've learned to play some music.

Ideas for Supplies ▼

- journal and pencil
- five-string banjo or guitar
- fingerpicks
- flat picks
- computer with microphone

MUSICAL NOTE

Earl Scruggs (1924–2012) was a legendary bluegrass musician. Scruggs was renowned for his three-finger banjo style, today called the "Scruggs style." With picks on the thumb, index, and middle finger, Scruggs plucked upwards. Lightning-quick finger "rolls" created syncopated licks. His banjo banged out the driving beat of bluegrass. Watch Earl Scruggs's fantastic fingerpicking action with the classic instrumental, "Foggy Mountain Breakdown."

Chapter 5 ▶
War and Social Change: Patriotism and Protest

Do epic conflicts produce epic music?

The Roaring Twenties came to an end with the crash of the stock market in 1929 and the onset of the Great Depression. Gone was the exuberance and creative energy of the 1920s as people struggled to feed their families and keep their homes.

Over the following decades America became involved in large-scale military conflicts around the world. After the global conflict of World War II in the 1940s, came the battles against communism in Southeast Asia during the Korean and Vietnam Wars in the 1950s and 1960s. With the ups and downs of war, moods shifted from feelings of pride and unity to anger and dissention.

Some artists performed patriotic tunes to improve morale both on military bases and at home. But while America was united by a sense of working toward a common goal in World War II and the Korean War, the Vietnam War deeply divided the country. By the 1960s, many sang out with protest messages expressing anti-war sentiments.

At the same time, the civil rights movement was in full force during the 1960s and 1970s. As President Obama said during a Black History Month event in 2010, the civil rights movement was a movement sustained by music, lifted by spirituals, and sharpened by protest songs that sang of wrongs that needed righting.

WORLD WAR II, 1939–1945

Worldwide depression and lingering resentment in Europe after World War I paved the path for World War II. Germany invaded one country after another beginning in 1939. At first America stayed out of the war, but when Japan attacked Pearl Harbor in Hawaii on December 7, 1941, it stunned the military—and all Americans. More than 2,000 Americans died and another 1,000 were wounded at Pearl Harbor. The following day, President Franklin D. Roosevelt declared war on Japan. Within days, he declared war on Japan's allies, Germany and Italy. America entered the deadliest war in human history, a war that led to over 70 million civilian and military deaths worldwide.

On the home front, many supported World War II. People worked together to ration food and gas, plant victory gardens, and finance the war effort by buying War Bonds. News of the war came over the radio and through newspapers. There was universal heartbreak as families throughout the country lost fathers, brothers, cousins, and uncles.

As in past wars, music provided relief from the stresses of war. But World War II was the first in history to occur during an age of mass-distributed popular culture. Music was a shared experience. People huddled around radios to listen to tunes that rallied troops on the front and lifted spirits at home. They sang war songs and danced the jitterbug and the boogie-woogie.

BLAST FROM THE PAST

In 1905, composer-playwright George M. Cohan (1878–1942) wrote the rousing patriotic march "You're a Grand Old Flag" for the stage musical *George Washington, Jr.* It became the first American song from a stage musical to sell a million copies. The song is still a classic.

In the 1942 film *Yankee Doodle Dandy*, James Cagney portrayed George M. Cohan, who was one of the most talented song-and-dance men in Broadway history. Cagney used Cohan's technique of half-singing and half-reciting songs. Released during the early days of American involvement in World War II, the patriotic film inspired pride and unity. Cagney received an Academy Award for his role.

PLAYLIST

In 2010, Katy Perry, Keri Hilson, and Jennifer Nettles harmonized a cover of "Boogie Woogie Bugle Boy," introducing the tune to a new generation of pop fans.

MUSICAL NOTE

For the third year in a row, over a billion dollars in Broadway theater tickets were sold in 2012.

Written in 1941, the Andrews Sisters' three-part harmony, "Boogie Woogie Bugle Boy" became an iconic song of the era. The light-hearted jump blues song tells the story of a "famous trumpet man from out Chicago way" drafted for military duty who is stuck with a bugle, an instrument without valves. He's even more saddened that he only uses it to toot the wake-up reveille. His sympathetic captain quickly drafts a band to jam with the bugle boy and they entertain their company with bluesy rhythms! The happy story offered hope to troops about to depart for war.

THE GOLDEN AGE OF BROADWAY

These years were the golden age of Broadway. Many hits ran for over 1,000 shows. There's nothing like the in-the-moment experience of live theater. Musical theater is an American art form. The mark of success in American theater is a run in one of the 40 professional theaters in the Broadway district of Manhattan.

The seeds of Broadway were planted as early as 1750 when a theater holding nearly 300 people opened for Shakespearean productions and ballad operas. All theater stopped during the Revolutionary War but after the war, the Park Theater opened with 2,000 seats. More theaters opened as minstrel shows and vaudeville grew, and Broadway was an attractive place to build theaters in the 1800s because real estate prices were cheap.

The play *Show Boat* debuted in 1927, a popular musical set on a Mississippi River showboat based on a bestselling book. Critics and audiences loved the show. This was the launch of Broadway as the place for the best theater. The show ran for a year and a half, with a total of 572 performances.

In 1943, Roger's and Hammerstein's *Oklahoma* opened during the midst of World War II. Set in the early 1900s in the Indian Territory that became Oklahoma, it presented a simpler way of life and an escape from war's cruel realities. Combining song and dance numbers with dialogue, it was a smash, running for five years and 2,248 performances.

With enormous success, Oklahoma built off the success of Show Boat as a "book musical." Instead of musical numbers linked with snippets of dialogue and wacky gags, these musical plays feature integrated songs and dances. Performers portrayed genuine characters and audiences connected with their joys and sorrows.

THE VIETNAM WAR AND CIVIL RIGHTS MOVEMENT

Unlike World War II, which was nicknamed the "just war," the Vietnam War was an unpopular conflict among many Americans, especially young people. During the era's rapid cultural changes, a generation gap split kids and parents. Kids rebelled against their parents' ways of life. A counterculture rose up to spread messages of peace and love.

Flashing peace signs and wearing strands of love beads, young people known as hippies took to the streets. They were committed to nonviolent protest and opposed the war. Their shocked parents had endured the hardships of the Great Depression and the sorrows of World War II. Many were patriotic veterans. They didn't understand their kids' behavior and their kids didn't understand why. Bridging the gap seemed hopeless.

BLAST FROM THE PAST

Woody Guthrie's 1940 beloved folksong, "This Land Is Your Land," is often considered a patriotic anthem. The song praises America's beauty and the chorus, "This land was made for you and me," expresses unity and love of country.

Many people aren't aware of a verse that presents a bleaker perspective of the time, one of unemployment and struggles to make ends meet.

In the squares of the city/In the shadow of the steeple

Near the relief office/I see my people/And some are grumblin'

And some are wonderin'/If this land's still made for you and me.

In 2009, Pete Seeger and Bruce Springsteen performed the full lyrics on the steps of Washington, DC's Lincoln Memorial.

The year 1969 marked the height of the hippie counterculture. In August, an estimated 500,000 hippies and others flocked to a dairy farm in upstate New York for a major moment in music history. Peaceful masses swarmed the Woodstock Art & Music Fair, which Canadian folksinger Joni Mitchell (1943–) called "a spark of beauty." Janis Joplin, Jimi Hendrix, The Who, Arlo Guthrie, Joan Baez, and others rocked Woodstock for three rainy days of peace, love, and free music.

Steven Van Zandt of the E Street Band lived the generation gap. He told *Time* magazine, "It's one of the few times in history where it was the dramatic shift between the past and the future, where the parents could not relate to the children."

In 1964, folksinger-songwriter and social activist Bob Dylan (1941–) sang "The Times They are a-Changin'." The anthem's lyrics, concerning issues of racism, poverty, and social change, still resonate:

The order is rapidly fadin'

And the first one now will later be the last

For the times they are a-changin'.

As the Vietnam War escalated and Dylan released his song, unrest gripped the nation. A disproportionate number of African Americans were drafted into the Vietnam War. Most of them experienced combat. A mass civil rights movement took a stand against segregation and discrimination in the South. As the 1960s rolled on, the women's rights movement gained momentum as well.

Musicians from all musical genres embraced the spirit of revolution. Protesters marched on Washington and belted out powerful hymns, including the freedom song "We Shall Overcome," which became the theme song of the civil rights movement. White folk artists, including Pete Seeger, Bob Dylan, Joan Baez, Janis Ian, and Phil Ochs sang of the shame of segregation and racism.

Jazz was so bound together with the civil rights movement that Martin Luther King delivered the opening address to the Berlin Jazz Festival in Berlin, Germany, in 1964. "Jazz speaks for life," King said. "The blues tell the story of life's difficulties—and, if you think for a moment, you realize that they take the hardest realities of life and put them into music, only to come out with some new hope or sense of triumph. This is triumphant music."

MOTOWN: HITSVILLE USA

Launched during the Civil Rights movement, the legendary Motown record label was the first label owned by an African American. It became a powerful source of cultural and social change, promoting black artists to mainstream, mostly white audiences. Motown Sound was uplifting and upbeat. With a blend of jazz, gospel, and traditional call-and-response, it introduced soul music to a mass audience.

Singer-songwriter Berry Gordy, Jr. (1928–) borrowed $800 from his family in 1959 and used it to turn his small Detroit home into a hit-making factory. The garage was the recording studio and the kitchen was the control station.

It didn't take Gordy long to sign his first group, Smokey Robinson and the Miracles. By 1961, the Miracles released Motown's first million-copy seller, "Shop Around." And the year kept getting better. The teen girl group, the Marvelettes, released "Please, Mr. Postman," which became Motown's first *Billboard* Hot 100 single and was later covered by The Beatles in 1963. With the Temptations' hit song "My Girl," and the Supremes' "Where Did Our Love Go?" Motown was officially mainstream. In 1968 the company had five records out of the Top 10 on *Billboard*'s Hot 100 chart.

Motown's upbeat sound united black and white, old and young. Diana Ross was the admiration of all teenage girls and the boys wanted to be just like Smokey Robinson. In the late '80s and '90s, all of Motown's major artists were inducted into the Rock and Roll Hall of Fame. When Gordy himself was inducted in 1988, he was given the following tribute: "Gordy endeavored to reach across the racial divide with music that could touch all people, regardless of the color of their skin." And he did just that.

How did Gordy come up with the name Motown? He replaced the "city" in Detroit's "Motor City" nickname with the more folksy, "town" to reflect his warm feelings about his community. Motor Town was soon shortened to Motown.

MUSICAL NOTE

It's no surprise Motown earned the nickname Hitsville USA. The label cranked out more than 180 No. 1 hits. Its stellar artists included Diana Ross and the Supremes, Smokey Robinson and the Miracles, Stevie Wonder, the Temptations, the Four Tops, Marvin Gaye, Michael Jackson and the Jackson 5, and Lionel Richie and the Commodores.

GET YOUR GROOVE ON! GRAVITY AND BALANCE IN DANCE

During World War II, dancing provided entertainment and an escape from the grim realities of the time. Dance is an art form, but physics is behind the moves! A force is a push or pull on an object. Gravity is one force that acts on all dancers to keep them balanced when they're in motion. Gravity pushes down on a dancer while the floor beneath the dancer's feet pushes up. How do dancers stay balanced? With subtle body shifts and adjustments. You can test a variety of body positions as you explore gravity and balance.

- **Consider some questions to explore**. You might consider: To stay balanced, where should your center of gravity be positioned? Will it be harder to balance if your feet are close together over a small section of the floor, or wider apart over a larger area? How should the body shift and adjust to stay balanced on one leg positioned to the back? To the front? When leaping? When spinning? Make predictions and formulate a hypothesis.

- **Decide what types of moves to test, and list them in the Move Executed portion of the data chart.** For example, you might test spins, leaps, and kicks.

- **Get your move on!** Take turns testing and spotting. The spotter should stand close enough to help if necessary but not too close to be an obstruction. As you test each move, note the position of your arms and legs. Measure the area you covered to execute the move. How did you make adjustments to stay balanced—or not. Dancers take tumbles all the time, even trained pros. Draw a simple diagram to illustrate body positions. What can you conclude from your tests? Evaluate your hypothesis.

Move Executed	
Position of Arms	
Position of Legs	
Area Covered	
Adjustments	
Diagram	

To investigate more, use a computer choreography program to create diagrams of dance moves. Use your discoveries and diagrams to choreograph a dance.

BOOGIE WOOGIE BUGLE

Tweens and teens in the 1940s jitterbugged to the cheery "Boogie Woogie Bugle Boy" of the Andrews Sisters. What kinds of sounds can you produce with your own bugle?

With your classmates, teacher, or parent, design an instrument. Explore the sounds you can produce with a bugle constructed of a length of garden hose and a funnel. Experiment with posture, breathing, and lip vibrations.

- **Before you begin construction, sketch a design.** Loop a section of hose in different ways to find a position that's comfortable for you to hold and maintain. Indicate where you will duct tape the hose in place. Note the funnel size you will use to create a bell at the end of the bugle. The larger the funnel, the louder the sound your instrument will produce. It's like a megaphone to amplify and spread notes. You will also need a mouthpiece. A soda bottle spout cut off the bottle works well. Can you think of other ways to make a mouthpiece?

- **Construct your bugle.** Duct tape works well to hold all the pieces together. What color duct tape did you choose? Do you want to decorate your bugle in any way?

- **Experiment with posture.** How does your bugle sound when you stand or sit straight and tall? How does it sound if you stand or sit in more scrunched-up positions? Try pressing your lips to the mouthpiece with different amounts of pressure. What makes the cleanest sounds?

- **Now, the trick is to buzz your lips to produce a sound like a "bzzz bee!"** If you're a brass player, demonstrate for others. You'll need to keep your lips moist to produce sounds—and that will collect saliva in the mouthpiece. Shake and wipe out the mouthpiece as needed. Your lips' vibrations will send a column of air into the bugle and out the bell to produce sound.

> To investigate more, design and construct bugles with funnels of different sizes. If you have a trumpet mouthpiece, test it. How do the sounds you produce differ and compare? Learn to play the reveille call or "Boogie Woogie Bugle Boy." Play along with other tunes, and invite other musicians to jam.

Ideas for Supplies ▼

- journal and pencil
- old garden hose
- knife
- plastic soda bottle
- funnel
- duct tape
- cloth to wipe out bell

KALEIDOSCOPIC EXTRAVAGANZA

During the 1920s, Busby Berkeley was a dance director for a number of Broadway musicals in which he arranged dancers into attractive geometric patterns. Throughout the 1930s and 1940s, he gained fame for creating spectacular human kaleidoscopic extravaganzas. A kaleidoscope is an optical device that uses reflected light to create dazzling symmetrical patterns.

What makes an object symmetrical? When it has the exact reflection on opposite sides of a dividing line. Consider rotational symmetry. If you rotate an object around a center point, at any angle from 0 to 360 degrees, presto! The object matches itself several times as it rotates. That's what happens as you spin a kaleidoscope.

Explore light's properties and the effects that angled mirrors create as you observe rotational symmetry with a homemade kaleidoscope.

🎵 Order of symmetry refers to the number of times an object looks the same in rotation. An object with no symmetry, like the letter R, is an order one. It must spin a full 360 degrees before it looks the same. An order two object is rotated halfway, to 180 degrees. Try it out. Write a large X on a sheet of paper. Draw a line of axis through it. Fold the paper lengthwise to the right along the axis, then lengthwise to the left. The X's halves should match both times because they are mirror images.

- **Before you begin construction, sketch a diagram for your own simple device.** You will want the three mirrors lengthwise with the reflecting sides facing inward. How can you attach them securely to form an equilateral triangle? A piece of wax paper at the bottom of the triangle makes a screen to look through. Arrange some shiny items on the white cardboard and hold the kaleidoscope above it to view them.

- **Observe rotational symmetry.** Sketch some of the designs. What happens as you rotate the mirrors? How many images do you observe? What happens when you rearrange the shiny items, or add different ones?

To investigate more, experiment with choreography. Use the sketches you created for inspiration. How can you orchestrate a kaleidoscopic arrangement like Busby Berkeley? View a Busby Berkeley production number from an old film. Watch a clip from the movie *Gold Diggers* of 1933. How are dancers arranged symmetrically? How does the whirling stage make moves kaleidoscopic? How does the camera angle allow the viewer to observe the beauty of symmetry?

Can you choreograph your friends or family members to use symmetrical arm and leg action to form images? Trying using props such as fans and feathers!

Ideas for Supplies ▼

- journal and pencil
- 3 flat, rectangular mirrors
- transparent tape
- rubber bands
- shiny items such as foil confetti, sequins, beads
- white cardboard

BLAST FROM THE PAST

The Beatles sang of a girl with kaleidoscope eyes in their 1967 classic "Lucy in the Sky With Diamonds." What's the story behind the ethereal music? Lucy O'Donnell was the song's famed Lucy. She attended Heath House nursery school with Julian Lennon (1963–), the son of singer-songwriter John Lennon (1940–1980). At the age of four, Julian created a drawing of his pal. Julian showed his artwork to his dad and announced, "That's Lucy in the sky with diamonds." The artwork ignited a flame of inspiration in the musician.

CHANGIN' TIMES:
SONGS OF SOCIAL PROTEST

Some protest songs of the Vietnam and civil rights era issued calls to action for social justice. Others, like the spirituals that preceded them, shared consolation and comfort. Many consider Bob Dylan's 1963 "Blowin' in the Wind" to be the most important protest song ever written. The song's melody borrows from the slavery-era folk song "No More Auction Block for Me." The lyrics pose questions about freedom, peace, and war, suggesting that things must and will change.

Listen to some protest songs and identify their themes and messages. Interpret the lyrics and determine whether each song is a call to action, a consolation, or an encouragement. Or does it contain another message?

Notable Quotable

"Deep in my heart, I do believe, we shall overcome."

—Dr. Martin Luther King, Jr., (1929–1968) in a brief speech just four days before his assassination in March 1968

MUSICAL NOTE

In 2004, *Rolling Stone* magazine put Dylan's "Blowin' in the Wind" at number 14 on its list of The 500 Greatest Songs of All Time.

- **What are some features to listen for in the songs?** Jot down your ideas.

- **Listen to and evaluate the songs in the data chart.** Can you find other protest songs to add to your list?

- **Share your observations about the songs and discuss the lyrics you noted.** What conclusions can you draw?

Song Title	Artist	Song's Purpose(s)	Evidence in Lyrics
We Shall Overcome	Pete Seeger		
We Shall Overcome	Joan Baez		
Blowin' in the Wind	Bob Dylan		
A Change is Gonna Come	Sam Cooke		
Keep on Pushing	The Impressions		
What's Going On	Marvin Gaye		

To investigate more, think about the ways the songs of the past can be applied to issues of today. How do the lyrics still resonate? What tweaks would you make in the lyrics to update them and call attention to a specific issue of the moment?

BLAST FROM THE PAST

Aretha Franklin (1942–) recorded "Respect" in 1967, which shot to the top of both the R&B and pop charts. Known as the Queen of Soul, her rendition of "Respect" was called the civil rights and feminist anthem of the time, symbolizing an appeal for respect and dignity. She sang the hymn "Precious Lord, Take My Hand" at Martin Luther King, Jr.'s funeral in 1968. More than 40 years later in 2009, Franklin sang "My Country 'Tis of Thee," a patriotic hymn written in 1831, at President Barack Obama's inauguration.

SING IN HARMONY

Motown artists the Temptations earned great success in the 1960s and '70s. Many consider them R&B and soul's most influential performers. One of the most successful bands ever, the Temptations boasted epic vocal harmonies that have sold tens of millions of records.

Work with your classmates, friends, or family members to explore vocal harmony.

- **Experiment with vocal ranges as you sing a series of octaves.** Who can sing at the highest, middle, and lowest pitch? Is there someone who can use the keyboard to establish the appropriate pitch for each note?

MUSICAL NOTE

The Temptations were also known for their sharp suits, smooth voices, and precision dance moves that included elegant and synchronized kicks, slides, and turns.

PLAYLIST

Visit the Motown Museum online. Explore the unforgettable Motown Sound. How about giving the Four Tops, Stevie Wonder, and the Temptations a spin? Listen to Motown's fantastic girl groups Diana Ross and the Supremes, Martha and the Vandellas, and the Marvelettes. Where do you hear influences of gospel and jazz? Which songs feature a call-and-response pattern?

- **Try a simple song, such as "Frère Jacques" or "Twinkle, Twinkle Little Star."** Sing in a parallel style. Invite the person with the middle pitch to sing the main melody. Blend your voices as you sing simultaneously. The voice taking on upper harmony sings one full octave above the middle pitch. The lower-harmony voice sings one full octave below. That way, voices will sound clearly different—and that creates harmony. If full octave differences aren't sung, the pitches won't be distinct and the sound can get muddled.

- **Record yourselves as you harmonize.** Listen to the playback, and assess your sound. Where do you need to make tweaks? What sounds great? Why? Can you make improvements? Record yourselves again and compare the two versions.

Ideas for Supplies ▼

- journal and pencil
- keyboard
- computer
- recording equipment

To investigate more, watch a performance of the Temptations beloved soul classic "My Girl" and listen to the incredible three-part harmony.

- Listen to the amazing arrangement of voices. David Ruffin sings lead in a sweet, smooth melody. The rest of the group tackles harmonic background vocals. When can you hear the lowest voice come in? The highest voices? How do all voices combine and blend? What impact does harmony have on the song?

- How does the chorus, "My girl, my girl, my girl/ Talkin' 'bout my girl/My girl" use harmony? How does harmony add emphasis to the meaning?

- Share your observations. Then, watch the performance again. Sing along with the Temptations. Choose one person to sing melody and the others to provide back up. Practice singing with your different pitches to combine your voices. Record your rehearsals and critique your sound.

Chapter 6 ▶
Rock and Roll Is Here to Stay

What makes rock music so popular?

🎵 In 1951, disc jockey Alan Freed began playing rhythm and blues music for a multi-racial audience in Cleveland, Ohio. He is credited with first using the phrase "rock and roll" to describe the music.

BLAST FROM THE PAST

Billboard Magazine started ranking the top singles in the music industry in 1948 and has published their rankings every week since. They look at how often the song is played on the radio or how many copies are sold. Today, they also factor in song streaming from the Internet.

In 2012, Americans made a record number of music purchases. What type of music did they choose the most? Rock! Topping the charts at over 102 million albums sold, even the next-closest type was still a subgenre of rock called "alternative," which sold 52.2 million albums.

Though today's rock sounds different from what first emerged in the 1950s, generations of artists have impacted the rock music you listen to today. Rock's guitar-jamming, piano-banging, sax-wailing pioneers, including Chuck Berry, Jerry Lee Lewis, Fats Domino, Little Richard, and Elvis, electrified audiences and influenced those that followed. With roots in blues, country, gospel, and R&B, rock and roll promises something for all tastes. Teenagers across racial, religious, and social lines all find a place in rock's eclectic universe.

Since about 1967, the term "rock" has been used to describe not only classic rock music itself, but also its many related styles, including rockabilly, folk rock, hard rock, soft rock, punk rock, and heavy metal.

THE BIRTH OF ROCK AND ROLL

After World War II, a youth culture emerged. Nearly 80 million babies were born between 1946 and 1964. This was the Baby Boomer generation and the era's kids hungered for music to call their own. Rock and roll careened onto the stage in the prosperous post-war era and its exhilarating hook never let go!

Baby Boomers claimed rock as their own. They were the first generation to grow up to the rhythms of rock and to grow up with TV. New forms of mass media meant rockers could get their music out to an enormous national audience. Kids listened to music on the radio, bought rock 'n roll records, watched *American Bandstand* in the afternoon, and went to movies featuring rock and roll music. Watching bands on TV became as popular as spinning vinyl on record players and cranking transistor radios. When people watched thrilling new artists on TV, the next day the same catchy tunes were "stuck" in millions of heads.

As rock evolved in the 1960s and 1970s, musicians navigated the rapidly changing times. The music they played reflected the conflicts young people had with an older generation, with society, and with the world.

What's behind rock's incredible staying power? It challenges each of us to explore our own role in society. Much of rock music's emotional power comes from its reflection of the search for who we are. Songwriters and artists strive to define themselves through their music and to inspire us to question the world around us and formulate personal beliefs.

PLAYLIST

Listen to songs from many types of rock music to understand how broad the category of rock is. With your parents, or with their permission, explore music from these well-known artists.

- **rockabilly**: Johnny Cash and Elvis Presley, Little Richard
- **folk rock**: Bob Dylan and Simon & Garfunkel
- **hard rock**: Led Zeppelin and the Who
- **soft rock**: Carol King and Cat Stevens
- **punk rock**: The Clash and the Ramones
- **heavy metal**: Metallica and Kiss

American Bandstand **was a popular show that ran from 1952 until 1989. It broadcasted teen styles, tastes, and music across the United States.**

♪ "Rock Around the
Clock" became the first
rock and roll single
to top the *Billboard*
charts. Over 25 million
copies have been sold
around the world.

CHUCK BERRY

In the late 1940s and early 1950s, R&B's strong backbeat, driving 4/4 time, and 12-bar blues laid tracks for rock and roll's rollout. In those days, kids listened to rock secretly, when parents weren't around. But by 1955, things looked very different.

Chuck Berry's (1926–) influence on rock and roll could be the greatest of all the early breakthrough rock and roll artists. Brian Wilson of the Beach Boys said, he wrote "all of the great songs and came up with all the rock & roll beats." Recorded in 1955, Berry's first single, "Maybellene" featured imaginative lyrics, a 24-bar guitar solo in the middle, and a thumping beat. It was promoted by disc jockey Alan Freed and embraced by white teenagers. His rock and roll classics, which include "Roll Over Beethoven," "Johnny B. Goode," and "Rock and Roll Music" have been covered by a wide range of artists, such as Elvis Presley, the Beatles, the Rolling Stones, the Beach Boys, Jimi Hendrix, and Bruce Springsteen.

Notable Quotable

**"If you tried to give
rock and roll another
name, you might call it
'Church Berry."**

—John Lennon,
The Beatles

BILL HALEY AND THE COMETS

In 1954, Bill Haley and the Comets released their exuberant, raucous single, "Rock Around the Clock." When the song was featured in the 1955 film *Blackboard Jungle*, it kicked up a frenzy that launched the rock revolution. A celebration of music and dance with a rockabilly beat, the song's lyrics boasted an unforgettable hook that foreshadowed rock's continuing popularity:

We're gonna rock around the clock tonight

We're gonna rock, rock, rock, 'till broad daylight

We're gonna rock, gonna rock around the clock tonight.

PLAYLIST

In 1974, the popular TV show *Happy Days* used "Rock Around the Clock" as its theme song and introduced the tune to a new generation of kids. Decades later, reruns of the popular show keep "Rock Around the Clock" rolling.

THE KING—ELVIS PRESLEY

This entertainment icon was one of the most popular artists of the twentieth century. He only needs one name—Elvis—and millions of people know exactly who it is. Elvis Presley (1935–1977), nicknamed "The King," has sold over 1 billion records worldwide.

Deeply influenced by gospel music, Elvis' energetic, uninhibited style embraced the joy of rock and delivered it to a larger audience. He fused several styles by vigorously blending southern folk music, country, and rock and roll. When it was "all shook up," he helped spread rockabilly to the masses.

To some people, Elvis represented the generation gap. Many blamed him for coming between kids and adults. Younger audiences swooned for Elvis' swagger and swivel-hipped dance moves that shocked their parents. With a slicked pompadour, a hairdo with a swirl over the forehead, and a rockabilly strut, he was a living, breathing symbol of what kids loved and parents feared. Preachers denounced Elvis from their pulpits and smashed his records.

BLAST FROM THE PAST

Like Elvis, Bill Haley and the Comets also made historic appearances on *The Ed Sullivan Show*. The weekly variety program that ran from 1948 to 1971 proved instrumental in helping new talent gain recognition. Early rock and roll legends, including Little Richard, Chuck Berry, the Beatles, and the Rolling Stones connected with millions of far-flung fans when they appeared on the show.

In the late 1960s, Janis Joplin (1943–1970) reigned as the "Queen of Rock and Roll." Her bluesy, raspy vocals and electric energy drove the rock classic "Piece of My Heart." Florence Welch (1986–), lead singer of indie rockers Florence and the Machine, studied videos of Joplin's wailing performances. Can you see and hear influences of Joplin in Welch's video of "Dog Days are Over?" Welch said, "Her connection with the audience was really important. It seems to me the suffering and intensity of her performance go hand in hand. There was always a sense of longing, of searching for something. I think she really sums up the idea that soul is about putting your pain into something beautiful. And that's why she's so important to me."

In 1956, Elvis gave an electrifying performance to 60 million people of all ages who tuned in to watch him on *The Ed Sullivan Show*. He belted out "Don't Be Cruel," crooned "Love Me Tender," and closed with "Hound Dog." As parents pushed back against rock even more, Elvis became more loved among millions of teenagers.

THE BRITISH INVASION

In the mid-1960s, music from British rock and roll bands spread to the United States and gave birth to a new age of rock.

By 1963, the Beatles had taken Britain by storm. That December, the single "I Want to Hold Your Hand" spent seven weeks as number 1 on the charts in the United States. When they came to New York in February 1964, 73 million people watched them on *The Ed Sullivan Show*. Two other British bands, the Rolling Stones and the Who, also became wildly popular.

Rolling Stone magazine named the Who's 1965 hit "My Generation" the 11th greatest song of all time. "My Generation" became an anthem of the generation gap.

Featuring a call-and-response, lead vocalist Roger Daltry sang, "People try to put us d-down," while Pete Townsend and John Entwhistle harmonized on backups, "Talkin' 'bout my generation."

THE 1970s AND BEYOND

The widespread move for change during the Vietnam War produced some of the era's best rock. Kids flocked to record stores to snag hot new releases. At home, they blasted vinyl on record players and stereos. After the war, a mix of hard rock and blues created a new sound made popular by Queen, the Eagles, David Bowie, Yes, and Led Zeppelin. Late in the 1970s, The Ramones combined teenage rage with rock and roll to launch the next huge movement in rock as punk music took center stage.

Generation X, the 46 million born from 1964 to 1980, hit their teen years in the 1980s and '90s. Gen-X rocked out to such an eclectic variety of sounds, it's hard to characterize the '80s by any one form of music. Heavy metal bands such as Guns and Roses, Van Halen, AC/DC, and Aerosmith took hold with their power ballads and wailing guitar solos. A punk, funk, disco mix called "new wave" was made popular by the B-52s, Talking Heads, and Blondie. Indie and alternative rock came along later in the decade with the Cure, R.E.M., and U2, and was the music of choice in Gen-X college dormitories. Expression of teenage angst continued in the 1990s when the Seattle grunge band Nirvana belted out their dark lyrics over strong guitar riffs with distortion and feedback.

While rock is one of the newer styles of music, its variety has given it the broadest appeal. Almost every rock band around today was influenced by rock and roll's true pioneers. If you haven't listened to a good Beatles song lately, you're missing out!

The word "indie" stands for independent and refers to diverse musicians and bands that are part of independent record labels. Popular on university radio stations, indie music is often called college rock.

MUSICAL NOTE

Patti Smith (1946–) is nicknamed the "Godmother of Punk." With passionate, poetic rock, the raw-voiced singer created compelling visual images through words. Her most widely known song, "Because the Night" reached number 13 on the charts in 1978. In *She's a Rebel: The History of Women in Rock and Roll*, Gillian G. Gaar writes, "Smith's biting delivery was something new for a female singer." Her audiences remain fanatically loyal.

PEOPLE HAVE THE POWER

Whether in protest songs or pure rock and roll, a song's lyrics implore us to consider the mood and issues of the day. They explore political, social, and religious identities. You can also use music to explore who you are.

- **Listen to the tunes on the Playlist here and others of your choice.** Some people respond to angry songs, while others prefer those that are gentle. Interpret the lyrics and evaluate different styles. What issues do the songs address? What emotions does the music stir? How do artists' voices and delivery styles impact their messages? Identify an issue facing the country or your own community today.

PLAYLIST

Rocker Bruce Springsteen's (1949–) classic "Born in the USA" is a passionate expression of the difficulties Vietnam War veterans faced when they returned home after serving their country.

U2's "Sunday, Bloody, Sunday." With its anguished tone and militaristic beat, it recalls the 1976 incident in Derry, Ireland, in which British police shot civil rights protesters.

Pete Seeger's mournful anti-war song, "Where Have All the Flowers Gone?"

Punk rocker and political activist Patti Smith's "People Have the Power," an optimistic song for hope.

* **Use it as a theme for an original composition.** Decide what kind of approach you will take—dreamy, defiant, sarcastic, serious, humorous, etc. You can present your composition as a poem, or set it to music.

Ideas for Supplies

* journal and pencil
* musical instruments
* music notation paper
* computer and music composition and notation program

To investigate more, listen to a variety of songs that address the quest for identity. Can you find common themes and messages? Listen to and evaluate lyrics from:

* "Just a Girl," which addresses female stereotypes, written by No Doubt's Gwen Stefani and Tom Dumont.

* "Waiting for My Real Life to Begin," which expresses a yearning for the future, by Colin Hay.

* "Still Haven't Found What I'm Looking For," a seeking song by U2.

Can you make a personal connection to the songs? Are there any songs that express similar feelings or questions you've experienced?

Compose a song about who you are or your own search to define yourself. Brainstorm issues you are passionate about. What contributions would you like to make to the world, big or small? What are your hopes and dreams for the future? Generate a word cloud to capture your ideas. Use it for inspiration. Write at least three verses with a chorus. Include a melodious hook to snag your listener's attention.

Notable Quotable

"Imagine all the people sharing all the world."

—John Lennon, "Imagine"

ROCKIN' ROBIN

Birds are nature's rock and roll musicians! With your teacher, classmates, or family, conduct a field study. Take a nature hike, and listen to the melodies of beautiful birdsongs. Record birdsongs and use them in an original composition. Can you duplicate the sounds with your own voice or with a musical instrument?

- **Consider questions such as the following: What are the rhythms of their sounds?** How do birds use pitch? How do birds respond to other calls? Discuss your ideas, and brainstorm additional questions. Make predictions. What methods and devices can you use to record birdsongs?

- **In the field, scout for multiple quiet locations where you can listen to birdsongs and make recordings.** Do you hear any other sounds, such as a woodpecker rapping against a tree trunk or the flapping of a great blue heron's wings? How are the sounds rhythmic? How can you use them as a backbeat?

- **After your field study, how can you analyze your data and evaluate your results?** Experiment with musical instruments and your voice to duplicate birdsongs. Arrange your recordings into an original composition. You can also upload recordings into a composition and notation program.

- **Rehearse your piece with your group and perform it for an audience.** Can audience members identify nature's influence?

BLAST FROM THE PAST

In 1958, R&B vocalist Bobby Day (1932–1990) topped the charts with "Rockin' Robin," by Leon René. The hit single's driving rhythm and bright, buoyant lyrics featured a catchy, "Tweedle-lee-dee-dee-dee" lead-in.

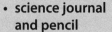
- science journal and pencil
- recording devices
- musical instruments
- music composition and notation software

To investigate more, explore an online source such as xeno-canto.org. This citizen science project shares worldwide birdsongs. Can you identify the birdsongs you heard, or confirm the species you listened to? View and listen to Bobby Day's 1958 performance of "Rockin' Robin." How does the song use a robin's chirruping and tweeting? Which instruments provide the birdsong? Check out the Jackson Five's 1972 cover of the same song. Which version more effectively employs the birdsong, and why? Compose and perform a hip-hop cover of "Rockin' Robin."

Chapter 7 ▶
The Age of Technology

How has digital technology changed music?

🎵 Hip-hop is widely popular in the United States, with artists including Jay Z, Eminem, Lil Wayne, Nicki Manaj, Eve, and Fergie topping the charts.

Today you live in an uber-connected world where the pace of new technology is daily news. The Millennial Generation includes 78 million people born from 1981 to 2000. In a generation still growing, kids born from 2001 to the present are described as Generation Z. These generations are the most racially and ethnically diverse in American's history.

Technology is an essential part of everyday life for these generations. These are kids like you who have grown up with text messaging, blogs, social networking, and more. With a swipe or a tap, you're connected. You can record a song and text it to a friend across town. Or shoot a video to send to a relative halfway around the world. You can download the music and watch the performances included in this book.

When did technology's incredible influence on the music scene amp up? Toward the end of the twentieth century, with rock's continued popularity and the birth of hip-hop. You may not remember a time before downloads, but that's when hip-hop began.

HIP-HOP'S FATHER

In 1973, a girl turning 16 wanted to raise money to buy clothes before starting school. She rented the recreation room of her apartment building and threw a party. Her brother, Clive Campbell, and his record collection provided the music. Three hundred people came to her "DJ Kool Herc Party," and everyone had a great time. By the next summer, Clive Campbell was playing outdoors at parks and in clubs in the Bronx. He started experimenting with two turntables and two copies of the same record, focusing on percussion and playing the drum sections of the albums one after the other. Vocals and other instruments were dropped out, creating a beat that people loved to dance to. At the same time he recited rhymes.

DJ Kool Herc (1955–) is the stage name of Jamaican-born artist Clive Campbell. He's a legend, and the father of hip-hop. In 1973, he began blasting a thrilling new genre into the music scene of New York from the streets of the Bronx. Campbell's family had immigrated from Jamaica where a sound system culture of technology created mobile discothéques of turntables, massive speakers, and charismatic DJs.

Like so many other immigrants, from colonial times to the present, Campbell transferred cultural memories to a new home. With roving dance clubs, Jamaican DJs shared American soul and R&B music along with their traditional reggae music. Toasting was a tradition in Jamaica. This chanting, or talking over a rhythm or beat, directly influenced hip-hop.

Notable Quotable

"Hip-hop never asked to change the world. But in its own noisy and stylish way it has done just that."

—S. Craig Watkins, *Hip-Hop Matters: Politics, Pop Culture, and Struggle for the Soul of a Movement*

Hip-hop music is the stylized rhythmic music that forms the background for rapping. Hip-hop culture is defined by rapping, DJing and scratching, break dancing, slam poetry, and beatboxing.

Hip-hop evolved from West African griot traditions brought to America by slaves. West African griots were wandering poets, storytellers, and musicians who shared traditional tales and sounds through the oral tradition.

MUSICAL NOTE

When freestyle rappers like Eminem and Jay-Z spit rhymes off the top of their heads, neuroscientists discovered that the brain's prefrontal cortex is hard at work. That's the portion of the brain that controls our drive and motivation. They also saw that the portions that act as our inner critic shuts off, letting our creative juices flow. When you create, turn off that pesky inner critic. Get lost in your creative energy. Get in the flow!

LIVE STREET PERFORMANCE

Hip-hop expanded throughout the 1970s, although it still remained contained in New York. At that time, rap was called emceeing. Artists performed live at massive block parties. At these raucous street celebrations, MCs were the opening acts for DJs, who provided the main attraction with scratching. Using their hands, DJs zigzagged vinyl LPs over turntables. It was a bold innovation. With a screech that demanded attention, scratching literally turned the tables on recorded music. It challenged people to listen up and reimagine rhythms.

Soon, the performing tables turned when the MCs seized center stage and DJs provided background accompaniment. MCs performed to the consistent beat of instrumentals, while DJs arranged compositions.

What is behind a rapper's rhythmic delivery and witty vocals? Storytelling pulses at the heart of hip-hop with stories that grab the listener. Like the wandering balladeers, spiritual singers, blues musicians, and protest singers who came before them, rappers have something to say. Audiences latched onto their messages of the struggles and difficulties of living in poverty in the inner cities, and the anger and sadness of social inequalities.

RAPID CHANGES

Kurt Walker (1959–) uses the stage name Kurtis Blow. In 1979, with his influence, rap exploded out of the underground scene. Hip-hop went mainstream when Blow became the first rapper signed to a record label, Mercury Records.

Collaborating with other pioneers, including Grandmaster Flash, Mele Mel, and Russell Simmons, Blow was the first rapper to go on a national and international concert tour. His 1980 song "The Breaks" hit gold. The musical melting pot of hip-hop flourished with mass media distribution in the same way rock did. By 1981, visuals and sound combined in the popular music videos kids watched on MTV. In 1982, the digital revolution brought CD players. Listeners played any genre on portable CDs as well as cassettes and vinyl. By 1998, music lovers were exploring the new technology of MP3 players.

The world seemed a hopeful place at the start of the new millennium. But radical changes and heartbreak came with the devastating terrorist attacks on the World Trade Center on September 11, 2001. By the end of 2008, millions had lost homes in the housing crisis. People struggled to find work in a dwindling job market while wars in Iraq and Afghanistan dragged on and on. Once again, music offered an escape and helped rally people for action.

Kids found refuge in music—and connectivity. They turned away from listening to music on the radio. They stopped browsing old-school records shops, because listeners could find access at their fingertips. By 2011, 45 million people paid for music downloads through services like iTunes, Pandora, Rdio, and Spotify. In 2013, Twitter's 20 million users gained access to Twitter #music, an amazing service that highlights hot tracks and emerging artists. As Twitter noted, "And, of course, you can tweet songs right from the app."

PLAYLIST

In 2002, classic rocker Bruce Springsteen shared sorrow and desperation with "The Rising." The mournful song is about a New York City fire fighter climbing into the devastated World Trade Tower.

In 2011, he lent his distinctive ragged vocals to Stewart Francke's "Summer Soldier (Holler if Ya Hear Me)." The mournful call-and-response tune addresses the ongoing war in Afghanistan that began in 2001.

In 2012, alternative singer-songwriter Beck released an unusual collection. *Song Reader* is a book of original songs written by Beck, but it includes only the sheet music. It is not a recorded album. You buy the book of music and the rest is up to you. It's a blast from the past when, as the innovative artist said, "The idea of sitting around a piano and playing a song with your friends and family was as much a part of our consciousness as Facebook is now." Musicians can post their own performances of the songs to the *Song Reader* official website. Renditions range from acoustic guitar instrumental versions to synthesizer-heavy techno-pop interpretations.

GOING GLOBAL

The music scene has changed rapidly with technology and its global transmission. In 2002, pop rock artist Kelly Clarkson won the first season of *American Idol*, a reality TV show that invites singers to compete for fame and a record deal with a major label. People all over the world vote after each show for favorites via text messaging, online, or with the *American Idol* app.

From 2008 to 2012, viral sensations including former busker Justin Bieber, "Call Me Maybe"s' Carly Rae Jepsen, and "Gangham Style"s' Psy and his horse dance experienced overnight international success. Today, instant access to downloads is our new normal. Listeners wear earbuds and toe-tap to personal playlists. We view music videos online and in our palms. We connect with artists through social networking, something unheard of not so long ago.

Not everyone is thrilled with the changes in ways we experience music. In 2011, rocker Jon Bon Jovi lamented the loss of a "magical, magical time." He told the U.K.'s *Sunday Times Magazine*, "Kids today have missed the whole experience of putting the headphones on, turning it up to 10, holding the jacket, closing their eyes and getting lost in an album; and the beauty of taking your allowance money and making a decision based on the jacket, not knowing what the record sounded like, and looking at a couple of pictures and still imagining it."

LONG AND WINDING ROAD

We've taken a long and winding road from *The Bay Psalm Book*, America's first book and first book of music. African traditions that collided and mingled with European ways of life in the New World spread deep and sprawling roots through many genres. They have stayed vibrantly alive in jazz and blues, rock, hip-hop, and more.

Part of our collective identity, all of this music reflects American history and heritage. Artists compose music to explore the time in which they live. From the sorrows of slave life to the unity of patriotism, from the struggles for equality and the soaring power of hope, these social, political, and religious influences shaped American life—and American sound.

Every generation faces change. But one thing remains the same. Music strikes a chord in its listeners. It has the power to touch emotions and stir the soul. It inspires action. It can overcome.

What's next in our musical evolution? Stay tuned. The times are always a-changin'.

Notable Quotable

"Hip-hop is the last true folk art."

—MC Mos Def (1973–)

I'LL FLY AWAY OH, GLORY!...

SAY WHAT? MONDEGREEN GAME

Have you misheard a song's lyrics? There's a word for that—mondegreen! It's the misinterpretation or mishearing of a phrase, such as a line in a poem or a lyric in a song. American writer Sylvia Wright coined the term. She misheard a lyric in "The Bonny Earl O'Moray," a Scottish ballad. "Laid him on the green" became "Lady Mondegreen."

A mondegreen gives lyrics a whole new and often hilarious unintended meaning. Pop and rap songs are especially misheard. Why? It's usually more about the artist's enunciation than the listener's auditory acuity. And the songs are fast! With your classmates and friends, design a mondegreen game.

- **What are some questions to consider?** What mondegreens have you experienced? Listen to songs to focus on misheard lyrics. What do you think causes you to mishear?

MUSICAL NOTE

Gavin Edwards is the author of three books of mondegreens. One is *'Scuse Me While I Kiss This Guy.* Sound familiar? It's misheard from the 1967 Jimi Hendrix classic "Purple Haze." What's the actual lyric? "Excuse me while I kiss the sky."

On an online archive of misheard lyrics, listeners share slips of the ear. One person misheard Linkin Park's "In the End." "Keep that in mind that I designed this rhyme" became, "Keep that in mind that lasagna's rhyme."

- **Brainstorm some approaches your game might take to challenge the listener.** Will you use recorded music? Sing lyrics? Design an animated computer game? Perform a takeoff of a TV game show like *Jeopardy*?

- **Conceptualize your game on paper.** Set and explain the parameters. How many contestants can play simultaneously? What are the rules? How will you tally points?

- **When the game is ready, invite contestants to participate.** Afterward, assess and evaluate the game. What changes can you make to improve it?

To investigate more, go beyond your group to ask others to share misheard lyrics. Incorporate additional mondegreens into your game.

Do you ever get a song stuck in your head? There's a word for that phenomenon—earworm! It comes from a translation of the German word *Ohrwrum*. Try adding earworms to your game.

Dr. Victoria William studies music psychology. She explains that earworm "refers to the experience of having a tune or a part of a tune stuck in your head. Often a person experiencing an earworm has no idea why a tune has popped into their head and has little control over how long it continues." It's a common phenomenon affecting over 90 percent of the population at least once a week.

Notable Quotable

"(Taylor) Swift writes perfect pop songs that stick in your head like lollipops stuck in your hair."

—Journalist Nancy Jo Sales

BODY BEAT BOX

Beat boxing, which is wildly popular with rap artists, is a form of vocal percussion. Its long, creative history is a celebration of spontaneity that dates to juba dancing. Explore the different sounds you can produce with just your body.

- **Test some techniques to create sounds with your mouth.** Inhale and exhale as a percussive device to establish a beat. Explore your articulators. Click your tongue against your palate. What kinds of sounds can you make with your mouth and lips? Imitate the whines and trills of musical instruments with your voice. Change pitches as you whistle. Work with a microphone to amplify and layer sounds.

Notable Quotable

"The beautiful thing about hip-hop is it's like an audio collage. You can take any form of music and do it in a hip-hop way and it'll be a hip-hop song. That's the only music you can do that with."

—Talib Kweli, alternative rapper

- **Test body percussion.** Rub, clap, and slide your hands together. Flick your finger with your thumb. What percussive sounds can you produce by thumping your chest, slapping your thighs, and stomping your feet? Can you think of anything else?

- **Select tunes from your personal playlist with which to keep percussive time.** Improvise with the songs. Try freestyling along with the beats, or recite a piece of poetry to the rhythm. What sounds surprised you? Which techniques worked best?

- **Record yourself on garage band one "instrument" at a time.** Can you sound like a whole band just using your vocals and body?

To investigate more, watch and listen to the artists listed below. Then use your discoveries to choreograph a juba dance and perform your own beatbox song.

- DeStorm Power is an Internet sensation who tackles multiple genres with complex, layered beatbox covers. Watch his covers of Michael Jackson's "Beat It," Bon Jovi's "My Life," and the holiday classic, "Carol of the Bells." Work with your group to have everyone contribute to layers of beatboxing as you cover a song of your choice.

- Stomp is a group that performs choreographed percussion. Let their exuberant moves inspire your own choreography.

- Listen to the astonishing instrument-free covers from Texas a cappella band Penatonix. How do the artists mimic instruments?

Notable Quotable

"The music I'm listening to was recorded to studio tape long ago, pressed to vinyl, digitized onto my home computer decades later, uploaded to iTunes Match, and streamed through the cloud to my laptop. Kind of cool when you think about it."

—Eric P.,
Facebook post

SHOWTIME!

This book has introduced you to many genres of music. You've learned about the history behind the different styles, and the way that music expresses the feelings of people, confronts the issues of society, and helps us understand current events. Music is fun and makes you want to move!

Work with your classmates, friends, or family to create, rehearse, and perform a live musical show. Include some of the genres you've explored in this book.

- **Jot down ideas and let your creativity fly as you collaborate.** Decide where you'll perform the show and what kinds of acts and numbers you'll include in the lineup. Which music genres will you feature? What kind of dances will you choreograph? Which instruments will you play? What production numbers will bookend the show's opening and finale?

- **Discuss ways that you'll publicize the show.** How can you invite an audience?

- **It takes time to get the show ready for performance.** Develop a rehearsal schedule to allow all performers to adequately prepare. How can you work together to rehearse your numbers? How can you share suggestions for improvement? Help one another gather or make costume pieces.

- **How do you want your performing space to look?** Have some fun with decorations and sets if you choose to use them.

MUSICAL NOTE

Some actors and musicians are superstitious. It's bad luck to say, "Good luck!" Before going on stage, actors and musicians tell one another, "Break a leg!" The origins of the phrase are murky. Some people believe it means a performer will put on such a fantastic show that he or she will snap a leg, taking bow after bow.

- **Determine the running order of the numbers and acts.** Design a program to distribute to the audience. Title each number, and include the names of the performers in each.

- **Conduct a final dress rehearsal before you perform for an audience.**

- **On the stage, enjoy the fun of creativity.** Break a leg!

To investigate more, look up one of your favorite artists and watch a live show online. What did they do to engage their audience? Why did they choose to perform those particular songs?

Ideas for Supplies ▼

- journal and pencil
- instruments
- costumes

GLOSSARY

a cappella: performed by voice only, without musical accompaniment.

abolitionist: a person supporting the end of slavery.

acoustic: music that is not electronically amplified.

acoustics: the scientific study of sound.

acuity: sharpness of hearing or sight.

African American: an American of African descent.

alliteration: the repetition of like sounds at the beginning of words in sequence.

alternative: a style of music that emerged in the late 1980s and early 1990s, which is characterized by bands with a do-it-yourself, non-conformist attitude.

alto: the second highest voice in a four-part chorus. It is typically the lowest female voice and the highest male voice.

amplify: to make a sound louder.

anonymous: not identified by name.

anthem: a song praising and declaring loyalty to something or a popular song that has become associated with a group, period, or cause that celebrates a sense of solidarity with it.

articulator: a moving or fixed organ involved in the sound-making process, including lips, tongue, teeth, and palate.

audible: loud or clear enough to be heard.

auditory: relating to hearing.

auditory nerve: the nerves that send impulses from the ear to the brain.

backbeat: a heavy, steady rhythm that stresses the second and fourth beats in a four-beat measure, often characteristic of rhythm and blues and other types of rock music.

ballad: poetic verses set to song.

balladeer: someone who performs ballads.

bar: a unit of time in music, divided according to the number of beats. Also called a measure.

baritone: a male voice with a range higher than a bass and lower than a tenor.

beat: an interval of measured time.

blues: a type of popular music that developed from African American folk songs in the early twentieth century. Its slow sad songs are performed over a repeating harmonic pattern.

boogie-woogie: a percussive blues piano playing in quadruple time, featuring improvisation.

Broadway: a group of theaters in the Times Square neighborhood of New York City that are considered to stage the highest level of theater in the country.

busker: a street performer.

casualty: someone killed or injured in battle.

center of gravity: the point at which gravity is concentrated.

civil rights: the basic rights that all citizens of a society are supposed to have, such as the right to vote.

Civil War (1861–1865): the war between the northern states and southern states that ended slavery and began the process of creating a more unified country.

civilian: someone not in the military.

cochlea: the spiral-shaped structure in the inner ear that sends signals to the auditory nerve.

collective identity: the characteristics of a group that make it unique.

colonial: relating to the years 1607 through 1776, when people from Europe settled in colonies in America. The colonial period ended when the Declaration of Independence was signed and the United States of America was formed.

commercial: relating to the buying and selling of goods or services, with the purpose of making money.

communism: a system of government in which a single party holds power and the state controls the economy.

composer: a person who writes music.

conductivity: the ability of an object or substance to transmit heat, electricity, or sound.

Confederate: refers to the group of southern slave states that seceded from the Union and formed their own government in 1861.

counterculture: a culture with values that run deliberately counter to the larger society.

country: popular music played on guitars and fiddles, based on traditional folk music from the South and cowboy music from the West. The songs express strong personal emotions.

cover: to record a new version of a song that was first sung or made popular by another performer.

cultural: relating to a culture or civilization, or to the arts.

culture: the beliefs and way of life of a group of people.

data: information, facts, and numbers.

decibel: a unit used to measure the loudness of a sound.

democracy: a government elected freely by the people.

digital: involving the use of computer technology.

disco: a style of pop music with a steady pronounced beat, popular in the 1970s for dancing. It developed from soul music, in response to the growing popularity of discos.

dissention: to disagree with a widely held opinion.

diversity: when many different people or things exist within a group or place.

DJ: a disc jockey, someone who plays recorded music.

download: to transfer data from one digital device to another.

eclectic: from a variety of sources or styles.

embellish: to add detail or decoration. In music, to add extra notes, accents, or trills to a melody to make it more beautiful or interesting.

embouchure: the mouthpiece of a wind instrument and the positioning of the lips, tongue, and facial muscles when playing an instrument.

emotion: a strong feeling about something or somebody.

enduring: long lasting.

enhance: to make greater.

escapism: entertainment that allows people to take a break from life's harsh realities.

ethnically: relating to a group of people who share a common national, racial, or religious background.

falsetto: a singing voice that extends higher than a singer's normal range.

field holler: an agricultural work song created during the slave era, which involved call-and-response patterns sung while working at a particular, often synchronized pace.

fife: a wooden, high-pitched flute commonly used in military and marching military groups.

flapper: a fashionable young woman in the 1920s who wore short skirts and a short hairstyle, listened to jazz, and often behaved in ways not considered acceptable at the time.

flourish: to add a special element to something.

flow: a total immersion in creative expression with no inhibitions or self-criticism.

GLOSSARY

folk: traditional, narrative songs that common people pass down in the oral tradition. Folk is a form of music that expresses the struggles of the time and in which everyone is welcome to participate.

folk rock: a musical genre combining elements of folk and rock music.

forbearance: patience and tolerance in a difficult situation.

force: a push or pull acted upon an object.

frequency: the number of sound waves that pass a specific point each second.

friction: the rubbing of one object against another.

funk: a popular music genre that derives from jazz, blues, and soul. It is characterized by a heavy rhythmic bass and backbeat.

garage rock: a type of music prevalent in the 1960s that was more aggressive than was common at the time, often with growled or shouted vocals that dissolved into incoherent screaming.

generation gap: the difference in attitudes, behavior, and interests between people of different generations, especially between parents and their children.

genre: a category of artistic work.

geographical: relating to the features of the land.

gospel: religious music.

gramophone: an antique record player.

graph: a diagram used to show the relationship between two quantities that vary.

gravity: a physical force that draws bodies toward the center of the earth.

griot: a wandering poet or storyteller in West Africa.

grunge: an alternative rock form of the 1980s and 1990s characterized by heavily distorted electric guitars and apathetic or angst-filled lyrics.

hard rock: a form of loud, aggressive rock music that emphasizes electric guitar used with distortion and other effects.

harmony: a pleasing blend of two or more tones.

heavy metal: a highly amplified, harsh-sounding rock music with a strong beat.

heritage: the art, buildings, traditions, and beliefs that are important to a country's or the world's history.

hip-hop: a form of popular culture originating in the African American inner city areas, characterized by rap music, graffiti art, and breakdancing.

hook: a musical idea that attracts attention and the listener's ear.

hymn: a religious song of praise and worship.

hypothesis: an unproven idea that tries to explain certain facts or observations.

iconic: describes something that is famous for or symbolizes an idea, group of things, or period of time.

identity: the characteristics that somebody recognizes as belonging uniquely to himself or herself, that describes individual personality for life.

illiterate: not able to read or write.

immigrate: to move to a foreign country to live there permanently. An immigrant is a person who immigrates.

improvisation: created and performed without preparation. Music composed, sung, and played without planning or rehearsal.

indentured: commited to serve a master or employer for free for a certain period of time, often to pay a debt.

independence: being in control of your own country, government, or actions.

indie: a small independent business, especially related to music or film.

individualism: the pursuit of personal happiness and independence rather than goals or interests of a group.

industrial: related to manufacturing.

inequality: differences in opportunity and treatment based on social, ethnic, racial, or economic qualities.

injustice: unfair treatment of someone.

inspirational: affecting your emotions or giving you the enthusiasm to do or create something.

instrumental: for musical instruments, not voices.

intensity: the strength, power, or force of something.

jazz: popular music that originated among African Americans in New Orleans in the late nineteenth century. It is characterized by syncopated rhythms and improvisation. Jazz originally drew on ragtime, gospel, black spiritual songs, West African rhythms, and European harmonies.

juba: a dance style created by slaves that is accompanied with rhythmic hand-clapping and thigh and knee slaps.

jump blues: uptempo blues featuring horns that was a forerunner of R&B.

kaleidoscopic: a changing form or pattern in a symmetrical way as it occurs in a kaleidoscope.

landlord: a property owner who rents out land or housing.

lip synch: to move your lips along with a recorded speech or song.

lyrics: the words to a song.

mainstream: the prevailing thoughts, influences, or activities of a society or a group.

martial: related to war, soldiers, and military life.

measure: a unit of time in music, divided according to the number of beats. Also called a bar.

megaphone: a funnel-shaped device used to direct and amplify the voice or other sound.

melancholy: feeling or making someone feel a thoughtful sadness.

melodramatic: dramatic, sentimental, and highly emotional.

metaphorical: using a word or phrase that normally means one thing to mean something else, such as "a sea of trouble".

meter: rhythmic lines of verse.

middle class: the section of society between the poor and the wealthy, including business and professional people and skilled workers.

migration: moving from one place to another.

mimic: to copy something.

minstrel: a traveling musician or an entertainer in a variety show.

molecule: a tiny particle that combines with other molecules to make up air, water, rocks, you—everything.

momentum: the speed or force of an object's forward movement.

monopoly: control by one company or party.

MP3: a computer file standard for downloading compressed music from the Internet.

muffle: to make a sound less loud or distinct.

music: a creative, artistic arrangement of sound.

narrative: a story or account of events.

national anthem: a patriotic song that honors the history, traditions, and struggles of its people, which is either recognized officially by the government or unofficially through use by the people.

national heritage: the art, buildings, traditions, and beliefs that are important to a country's history.

New World: the land now made up of North and South America. It was called the New World by people from Europe because it was new to them.

GLOSSARY

noodle: to improvise on a musical instrument in a random way, often to warm up.

notes: arrangements of musical sounds in a specific order.

octave: the rhythmic grouping of eight tones, or the interval between the first and eighth tones on the musical scale.

oral tradition: passing stories, songs, and histories from one generation to another by mouth rather than in writing.

origin: the source of where something came from or where it began.

palate: the roof of the mouth.

parlor music: popular music played at home by members of the family.

patriotic: a feeling of devotion to and love for one's country.

patriotism: devotion to and love for one's country.

percussive: something that is hit.

perforate: to make a hole in something.

persecute: to cause harm or suffering to someone, often because of race or political beliefs.

phonograph: a machine that picks up and reproduces the sounds that have been recorded in the grooves cut into a vinyl record.

physics: the study of physical forces, including matter, energy, and motion.

physiology: the study of the internal workings of living things.

pinna: the external portion of the ear.

pitch: how high or low a sound is, depending on its frequency.

pop: modern commercial music, usually tuneful, uptempo and repetitive. Pop is aimed at the general public and the youth market in particular.

popular culture: cultural activities or commercial products reflecting or produced for the general masses of people.

precursor: something that comes before another of the same kind.

production number: a special musical routine performed by an entire cast, including singers, dancers, comics, etc.

prolific: producing many works.

protest: a statement or action expressing disapproval of or objection to something.

Psalm: a sacred song or poem of praise, especially from the Book of Psalms from the Bible.

punk rock: a fast, hard-edged music popular in the 1970s, typically with short songs, stripped-down instrumentation, and often political, anti-establishment lyrics.

R&B: rhythm and blues, a popular music style that combines jazz and blues with a strong backbeat.

racially: relating to race.

racist: hatred of people of a different race.

ragtime: a popular genre of the early 1900s, with a syncopated melody and an accompaniment of regular accents.

rap: spoken or chanted lyrics that rhyme, performed in time to a beat.

raspy: a rough, scratchy sound.

ration: limiting the amount of something to be used each week or month.

raucous: harsh and loud noise.

rebel: to fight against authority or someone fighting against authority.

rebellion: defying authority or an organized attempt to overthrow a government or other authority.

refrain: a line or group of lines repeated at the end of each verse. Also called the chorus.

reggae: Jamaican music featuring off-beat rhythmic accents.

resist: to refuse to do something.

resonance: the sound produced by a vibrating object.

reveille: a bugle call or trumpet call most often associated with the military. Mainly used to wake military personnel at sunrise.

Revolutionary War (1776–1783): the war between the colonies and the British government that ended with independence from England and the creation of the United States of America.

rhyme scheme: a pattern of rhyming lines in a poem. Letters such as a-b-c-a illustrate the way the lines rhyme.

rhythm: a regular pattern of beats in a musical piece.

riff: a repeated series of notes.

roadhouse: an inn, restaurant, or nightclub located on a road outside a town or city.

rock: a style of pop music, derived from rock and roll, usually played on electric or electronic instruments and equipment.

rock and roll: pop music derived from blues music that has heavily stressed beats. It is usually played on electric instruments and has simple, often repetitive, lyrics.

rockabilly: an early style of rock and roll music dating to the 1950s that combines elements of country, R&B, and bluegrass.

sacrifice: to give something up for the sake of something else.

salvation: deliverance from harm, ruin, or loss.

satirical: relating to literary wit that makes fun of people, their vices, and foolish behavior.

scale: a series of musical notes.

scat: a vocal improvisation common in jazz, often using only sounds and no words at all.

scratching: a DJ technique that involves producing sounds with vinyl records on turntables.

secular: not religious.

segregation: the practice of keeping racial, ethnic, or social groups separate.

sensation: a physical feeling.

self-expression: the communication of your own personality, feelings, or ideas, often through speech or art.

sharecropper: a farmer who works on someone else's land and receives a small share of a crop's value after paying for tools, seeds, housing, etc.

sinuses: cavities filled with air between the face and the skull.

social injustice: when people are treated unequally within a society.

society: an organized community of people.

soft rock: often derived from folk rock, using acoustic instruments and putting more emphasis on melody and harmonies.

soprano: the highest register of the female voice or a boy's voice.

soul: a combination of gospel and R&B music.

sound wave: invisible vibrations in the air that you hear as sound.

spiritual: a religious song arising from slavery that was inspired by the Old Testament of the Bible.

spontaneous: happening without planning.

stanza: a group of lines forming the basic recurring unit in a poem or song.

GLOSSARY

stereotypical: an overly simplified image of a person or group.

superfluous: unnecessary, or more than enough.

symmetry: in mathematical terms, corresponding in size, shape, and positions on both sides of an axis. In artistic terms, beauty in form based on balance.

synchronize: to occur at the same time.

syncopated: a musical rhythm that puts a stress on beats that are usually not stressed.

synthesizer: a device that generates electronic music or modifies sounds electronically.

techno: electronic dance music with a quick tempo created by digitally synthesized instruments.

technology: tools, methods, and systems used to solve a problem or do work.

tempo: the pace at which a musical piece is played, typically indicated on a composition.

toasting: chanting or talking over a rhythmic beat.

tone: the specific quality of musical sound.

Top 40: the most popular songs each week.

transverse: a flute held horizontally, not vertically like a recorder.

tympanic membrane: the thin layer of connective tissue in the ear, commonly called the eardrum.

Underground Railroad: a secret network of safe houses and people who helped slaves escape from slavery in the South. The Underground Railroad brought people to the North and Canada where slavery was not legal in the years before the American Civil War.

Union: the term used for the federal (national) government of the United States in the Civil War, which also referred to the northern states.

universal: used or understood by everyone.

upbeat: cheerful.

uprising: an act of rebellion or revolt against authority.

uptempo: having a quick-moving tempo, or pace.

urban: relating to a city.

variation: a different version of an original poem or song.

vaudeville: wildly popular entertainment in the late nineteenth and early twentieth centuries, which featured a variety of comedy acts, singers, musicians, and dancers.

velocity: the speed at which something moves and in what direction.

vibrate: to move back and forth quickly.

vibration: a back-and-forth movement.

victory garden: a garden planted by American civilians during World War II. About 2 million victory gardens produced 40 percent of the food grown in the United States during the war.

Victrola: a popular brand of antique record player.

vocal cord: one of two membranes stretched across the larynx through which air passes in the process of making sound.

vocal range: the measure of the range of pitches your voice can make.

vinyl: plastic records played on phonographs.

vulgar: crude or obscene, or poorly behaved.

▾ RESOURCES

↳Books

Record Store Days: From Vinyl to Digital and Back Again.
Calamar, Gary and Phil Gallo. Sterling, 2009.

Woodstock: Three Days That Rocked the World
Evans, Mike and Paul Kingsbury, eds. Sterling, 2009.

The Recording Secrets Behind 50 Great Albums.
Gorden, Kylee Swenson, ed. Back Beat Books, 2012.

Raggin', Jazzin', Rockin': A History of American Musical Instrument Makers.
VanHecke, Susan. Boyds Mills, 2011.

↳Websites

American Treasures of the Library of Congress
www.loc.gov/exhibits/treasures/

John F. Kennedy Center for the Performing Arts
www.kennedy-center.org

Mariner's Museum: Captive Passage
http://marinersmuseum.org/sites/micro/captivepassage/index.html

Memphis Rock 'n' Soul Museum
http://memphisrocknsoul.org/

National Music Museum
http://orgs.usd.edu/nmm/galleries.html

Patriotic Melodies, the Library of Congress
http://lcweb2.loc.gov/diglib/ihas/html/patriotic/patriotic-home.html

Rock and Roll Hall of Fame
www.rockhall.com

Transatlantic Slave Trade Database:
http://slavevoyages.org/tast/index.faces

Turner Classic Movies:
www.tcm.com

▾ INDEX